BTEC

First Applied Science:
Principles of Applied Science

UNIT 1 REVISION GUIDE

BTEC AWARD

Jo Locke

 Nelson Thornes

Published in 2012 by:
Nelson Thornes Ltd
Delta Place
27 Bath Road
CHELTENHAM
GL53 7TH
United Kingdom

12 13 14 15 16 / 10 9 8 7 6 5 4 3 2 1

A catalogue record for this book is available from the British Library

ISBN 978 1 4085 1842 7

Cover photograph: Fuse/Getty
Illustrations by Wearset Ltd and David Russell Illustration
Page make-up by Wearset Ltd, Boldon, Tyne & Wear
Printed and bound in Spain by GraphyCems

Photo acknowledgments

Page 1 Martyn F. Chillmaid; A13.1 David McCarthy/Science Photo Library; B4.1
iStock; D5.1 Sawayasu Tsuji/iStock; D5.2, D8.1, D10.1, D11.1, D11.2, F1.3 Andrew
Lambert Photography/Science Photo Library; D5.3 Martyn F. Chillmaid/Science
Photo Library; D5.4 Tatiana Goydenko/iStock; E1.1 microgen/iStock; E1.2 Modern
Design/Alamy; E1.3 Fenton/Fotolia; E1.4 isabelle limbach/iStock; E1.5 Robert
Kyllo/iStock; E1.6 tomas/Fotolia; E2.1 chris beddoe/iStock; E2.2 Brian Jackson/
Fotolia; E2.3 Nikola Miljkovic/iStock; E2.4 Jiri Snaidr/iStock;
E2.5 BrianHolmNielsen/iStock; E2.6 Paul McKeown/iStock; E3.1 jaileybug/Alamy;
E3.2 George Clerk/iStock; E4ab.1 Ida Jarosova/iStock; E4ab.2 Michael Valdez/
iStock; E4de.1 Paul Wilkinson/iStock; E4f.1 manuel velasco/iStock; E6a.1, F5ab.2
luoman/iStock; E6a.2 Nikola Miljkovic/iStock; E6a.3 Martin Bond/Science Photo
Library; F3.2 Darren Pullman/iStock; F4ab.1 Hadel Productions/iStock; F4cd.1 Dr.
Arthur Tucker/Science Photo Library; F4ef.1 itsjustme/iStock; F4g.1 Christopher
Badzioch/iStock; F4g.2 Custom Medical Stock Photo/Science Photo Library;
F5ab.1 Imgorthand/iStock; F5cd.1 selimaksan/iStock; Exam Q E1 t_kimura/iStock;
Exam Q F2 Custom Medical Stock Photo/Science Photo Library.

Unit 1 Principles of Science

Contents

Welcome to BTEC Principles of Applied Science!   1

A Explore cells, organs and genes   2

A.1   The basic structure, function and adaptations of cells   2
A.2   The function of the components of cells   4
A.3   Cells, tissues and organs   6
A.4   The functions of plant organs   7
A.5   Transpiration   8
Summary questions   9
A.6   DNA   10
A.7   Chromosomes and genes   11
A.8   Alleles   11
A.9   Monohybrid inheritance   12
A.10   Pedigree analysis   14
A.11   Genotypes and phenotypes   16
A.12   Calculating the likelihood of offspring displaying a particular characteristic   18
A.13   Gene mutations   20
Summary questions   21
Examination-style questions   22

B Explore the roles of the nervous and endocrine systems in homeostasis and communication   24

B.1   Homeostasis   24
B.2   Structure of the nervous system   25
B.3   Voluntary and involuntary responses   26
B.4   Transmission of electrical impulses along neurones and chemical transmission across synapses   26
B.5   Reflexes   28
Summary questions   30
B.6   The endocrine system   31
B.7   The endocrine and nervous system   32
B.8   Blood glucose concentration   32
B.9   Maintaining body temperature   34
Summary questions   35
Examination-style questions   36

C Explore atomic structure and the periodic table   38

C.1   Metals and non-metals   38
C.2   Structure of the atom   39
C.3   Nucleus of an atom   40
C.4   Atoms of elements   41
C.5   Atomic definitions   42
C.6   Subatomic particles   42
C.7   Numbers of subatomic particles   43
Summary questions   44
C.8   The periodic table   45
C.9   Isotopes   46
C.10   Relative atomic mass of isotopes   46
C.11   Calculating the relative atomic mass of isotopes   47
C.12   Electron shells   48
C.13   Groups on the periodic table   50
Summary questions   51
Examination-style questions   52

D Explore substances and chemical reactions   **54**

D.1	Using the periodic table to recognise elements and formulae of simple compounds	54
D.2	Elements, compounds, mixtures and molecules	55
D.3	Word equations	56
D.4	Balanced chemical equations	57
D.5	Reactions with acids, alkalis and salts	58
D.6	Acids, bases and alkalis	59
Summary questions		60
D.7	Neutralisation	61
D.8	Reacting acids and metals	62
D.9	Reacting acids and carbonates	63
D.10	Chemical tests for hydrogen and carbon dioxide	64
D.11	pH tests using universal indicator and litmus	65
D.12	Hazard symbols	66
D.13	Uses of neutralisation	67
D.14	Common chemical formulae	68
Summary questions		69
Examination-style questions		70

E Explore the importance of energy stores, energy transfers and energy transformations   **72**

E.1	Forms of energy and their uses	72
E.2	Energy stores and their uses	74
E.3	Energy transfers	76
Summary questions		78
E.4ab	Energy transfer – the conservation of energy	79
E.4c	Energy transfer – Sankey diagrams	80
E.4de	Energy transfer – power	81
E.4f	Energy transfer – the cost of electricity	82
E.5	Efficiency	83
E.6a	Sources and storage of energy – renewable	84
E.6b	Sources and storage of energy – non-renewable	86
E.6c	Sources and storage of energy – using energy stores effectively	87
E.6d	Sources and storage of energy – storage of energy	88
Summary questions		89
Examination-style questions		90

F Explore the properties and applications of waves in the electromagnetic spectrum   **92**

F.1	Wave characteristics	92
F.2	Wave calculations	94
F.3	The electromagnetic spectrum	96
Summary questions		98
F.4	Uses of waves in the electromagnetic spectrum	
F.4ab	Uses of radio waves and microwaves	99
F4cd	Uses of infrared and visible light	100
F.4ef	Uses of ultraviolet and X-rays	101
F.4g	Uses of gamma rays	102
F.5ab	Dangers of electromagnetic radiation – microwaves and infrared	103
F.5cd	Dangers of electromagnetic radiation – ultraviolet, X-rays and gamma rays	104
Summary questions		105
Examination-style questions		106

How to revise	108
How to answer questions	109
Science skills	110
Boost your Grade	
Formulae you need to learn	112
Formulae you need to know how to use	113
Answers	114
Glossary	119
Index	123

Welcome to BTEC Principles of Applied Science!

This book covers everything you need to revise for your Unit 1 Principles of Science exam and is packed full of features to help you achieve the very best that you can.

Key words are highlighted in the text and are shown **like this**. A glossary of these terms can be found on page 119.

⟶ *These questions check that you understand what you're learning as you go along. The answers can be found in the text and diagrams you have just read.*

Many diagrams are as important for you to learn as the text, so make sure you revise them carefully.

Exam tip

Exam tips are hints giving you important advice on things to remember and what to watch out for.

Bump up your grade

How you can improve your grade – this feature shows you where additional marks can be gained.

Halfway through, and at the end of each Learning aim you will find:

Checklist

Use the checklists to monitor your progress. Only move on to the next section once you have achieved three ticks for each topic.

Summary questions

These questions will test you on what you have learned throughout the Learning aim so far, helping you to work out what you have understood and where you need to go back and revise. The questions are colour-coded in terms of increasing difficulty, from green through to blue and then pink.

And at the end of each Learning aim you will find:

Examination-style questions

These questions are examples of the types of questions you will answer in your actual exam, so you can get lots of practice during your course. They are also colour-coded for difficulty level.

You can find answers to the Summary and Examination-style questions at the back of the book.

A.1

The basic structure, function and adaptations of cells

Cells are **specialised** to carry out a particular function. This means their structure is adapted to enable them to perform their job. You need to learn about the following cells:

Animal cells

Motor and sensory neurones

Neurones are nerve cells. They carry electrical impulses from one part of the body to another. Sensory neurones have receptors, which detect stimuli like light and sound. They transmit impulses from receptor cells to the central nervous system (CNS). Motor neurones carry impulses from the CNS to the effectors – muscles and glands.

Neurones are adapted by being:
- long and thin – so they can transmit impulses over long distances
- covered in fat – which acts as insulation, preventing the impulse signal being scrambled.

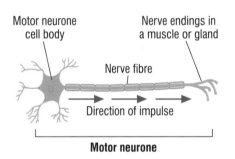

Motor neurone cell body — Nerve endings in a muscle or gland

Nerve fibre

Direction of impulse

Motor neurone

Nerve fibre — Sensory neurone cell body — Nerve endings in central nervous system

Sensory receptor — Direction of impulse

Sensory neurone

▷ **1** *What is the difference between a motor neurone and a sensory neurone?*

Red blood cell

Red blood cells carry oxygen around the body. They are adapted by:
- containing **haemoglobin**, a red pigment – this binds to an oxygen molecule
- having a disc-like shape – this maximises the surface area and allows more oxygen to be absorbed
- having no nucleus – so the whole cell is full of haemoglobin.

▷ **2** *What does haemoglobin do?*

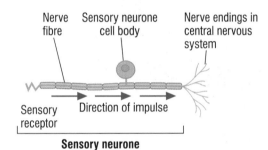

Red blood cell

White blood cell

White blood cells fight disease. There are a number of different types of white blood cell. They are adapted in different ways to do different things:
- change shape – this allows them to **engulf pathogens**
- produce **antibodies** – this allows them to attack microorganisms
- produce antitoxins – so they can destroy **toxins** produced by microorganisms.

▷ **3** *What does an antitoxin do?*

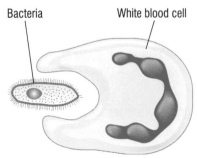

Bacteria — White blood cell

White blood cell engulfing a bacterium

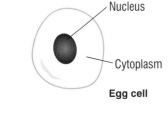

Egg cell

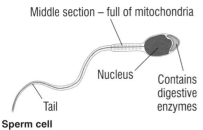

Egg cell

Egg cell

Egg cells are the female reproductive cells. Their job is to carry the female genetic material and to nourish the embryo as it starts to develop. They are adapted by having a store of food in the cytoplasm.

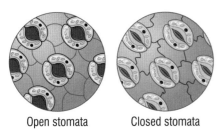

Sperm cell

Sperm cell

Sperm cells are the male reproductive cells. Their job is to carry the male genetic material to the egg. They are adapted by having:
- a long tail and streamlined head – so they can swim towards the egg
- enzymes in the head – to digest the egg cell membrane
- lots of mitochondria – to provide the energy needed to swim.

Plant cells

Root hair cell

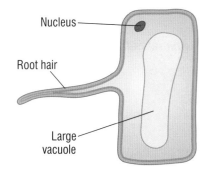

Root hair cell

Root hair cells absorb water and nutrients from the soil. They are adapted by having:
- a root hair – so there is a large surface area for absorbing water and minerals
- a large vacuole – this speeds up water movement from the soil into the root cell.

> **4** *Why does a root hair cell have a root hair?*

Xylem and phloem cells

The **xylem** and the **phloem** are responsible for transporting substances around the plant. The xylem carries water and minerals from the roots around the plant. In some plants the xylem also provides support. The phloem transports dissolved sugars from the leaves to the rest of the plant.

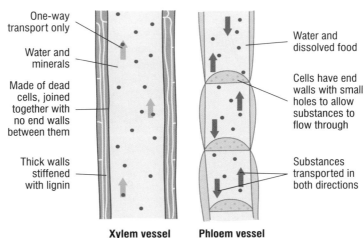

Xylem vessel   **Phloem vessel**

Adaptations of xylem and phloem

> **5** *What substances do the xylem vessels transport?*

Bump up your grade

You may find it easier to draw a diagram of a specialised cell and label its features, rather than writing about a cell type.

Guard cells

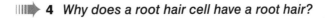

Open stomata   Closed stomata

Guard cells

Guard cells open and close **stomata** – tiny pores found on the underside of a leaf. The stomata allow gases to diffuse in to and out of the leaf – carbon dioxide diffuses **in** and oxygen and water vapour diffuse **out**.

Guard cells are adapted by being:
- able to change shape – this means the pores can open and close
- sensitive to light – the pores close at night, which saves water when the plant is not photosynthesising.

A.2

Key points

- The nucleus contains genetic information that controls the activities of the cell.
- The cytoplasm is where most chemical reactions take place.
- The cell membrane allows substances to enter and exit.
- Chloroplasts are the sites of photosynthesis.
- The cell wall provides structural support.
- The vacuole contains cell sap and provides extra support for the cell.
- Mitochondria are the sites of respiration.

Exam tip

If you are asked to explain the function of the nucleus, never say 'it is the brain of the cell'. This will achieve no marks. The nucleus controls what the cell does and contains genetic material.

The function of the components of cells

All living organisms are made up of tiny structures called **cells**. Cells are microscopic structures. They are so small that they can only be seen using a microscope.

Not all cells look alike, but they contain the same components.

▶ **1** *What piece of equipment would you use to see cells?*

Animal cells

Animal cells have four main components:

- **cytoplasm**
- **cell membrane**
- **nucleus**
- **mitochondria** (singular – mitochondrion).

▶ **2** *Name the four main components found in animal cells.*

Cytoplasm – this is a 'jelly-like' substance. Most chemical reactions in a cell take place here

Cell membrane – this is a barrier around the cell. It controls what can come in and out of the cell

Nucleus – contains the genetic information to decide what a cell will look like and what it does. It also contains the information needed to make new cells

Mitochondria – this is where **respiration** happens. Glucose and oxygen react and release energy

An animal cell

▶ **3** *Which part of the cell contains genetic information?*

Plant cells

As well as containing a nucleus, cytoplasm, cell membrane and mitochondria, plant cells have three other important components:

- **cell wall**
- **vacuole**
- **chloroplasts**.

4 *Name three components only found in plant cells.*

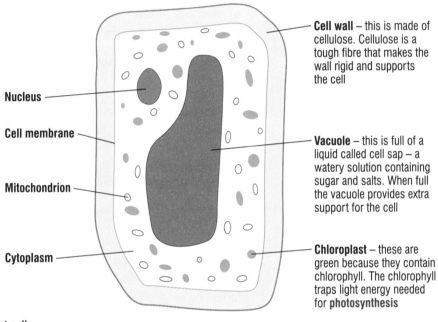

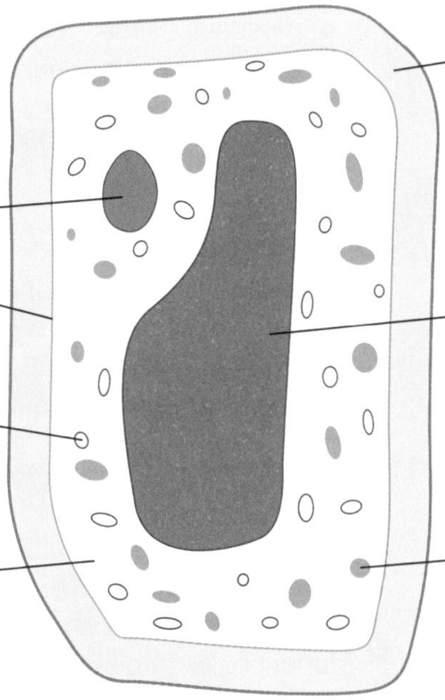
Nucleus
Cell membrane
Mitochondrion
Cytoplasm
Cell wall – this is made of cellulose. Cellulose is a tough fibre that makes the wall rigid and supports the cell
Vacuole – this is full of a liquid called cell sap – a watery solution containing sugar and salts. When full the vacuole provides extra support for the cell
Chloroplast – these are green because they contain chlorophyll. The chlorophyll traps light energy needed for **photosynthesis**

A plant cell

5 *What process occurs in the chloroplasts?*

6 *Where in a plant cell would you find cell sap?*

Key words: cells, cytoplasm, cell membrane, nucleus, mitochondria, respiration, cell wall, vacuole, chloroplast, photosynthesis

Exam tip

Make sure you learn how to spell key words such as 'cytoplasm' and 'chloroplast'. Mixing up these words will mean an examiner will have to mark your answer as wrong as they cannot be certain which component you are referring to.

Bump up your grade

If you are asked to 'compare' something in an exam question – for example the structures in plant and animal cells – try using a table to compare the features and then put a tick or cross to show whether the component is present, or not.

Component	Plant cell	Animal cell
Nucleus	✓	✓
Cytoplasm	✓	✓
Cell membrane	✓	✓
Chloroplasts	✓	✗
Cell wall	✓	✗
Vacuole	✓	✗
Mitochondria	✓	✓

A.3

Bump up your grade

Remember this simple flowchart to help you explain the levels of organisation within an organism:

cells
↓
tissues
↓
organs
↓
organ systems
↓
organism

Cells, tissues and organs

Bacteria and other single-celled organisms consist of only one cell. However to produce a fully functioning multicellular organism, such as a plant or an animal, many cells have to work together. Within multicellular organisms there are a number of levels of organisation.

Tissues

A **tissue** is made up of a group of specialised cells working together to perform a function. Examples of tissues include:

- muscular tissue – cells contract and relax to cause movement
- glandular tissue – makes and releases substances such as enzymes and hormones.

▶ **1** *What is a tissue?*

Organs

An **organ** is made up of different types of tissues working together to perform a function. Examples of organs include:

- stomach – involved in digesting food. It contains muscular and glandular tissue.
- heart – pumps blood around the body. It contains muscular and nervous tissue.

▶ **2** *What is an organ?*

Organ systems

An **organ system** is made up of a group of organs working together to perform a function. Examples of organ systems include:

- the digestive system – responsible for digesting food. It includes the stomach, intestines and liver.
- the excretory system – responsible for the removal of waste. It includes the kidneys, the bladder and the lungs.

Remember that an organ can be part of multiple systems. For example, the liver is involved in food digestion and also in removing toxins from the blood.

▶ **3** *What is an organ system?*

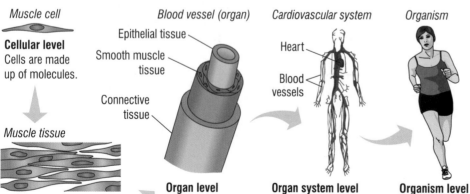

Levels of organisation in an organism

Muscle cell

Cellular level
Cells are made up of molecules.

Muscle tissue

Tissue level
Tissues consist of similar types of cells.

Blood vessel (organ)
Epithelial tissue
Smooth muscle tissue
Connective tissue

Organ level
Organs are made up of different types of tissues.

Cardiovascular system
Heart
Blood vessels

Organ system level
Organ systems consist of different organs that work together closely.

Organism

Organism level
The human organism is made up of many organ systems.

Organism

An **organism** is made up of a group of organ systems working together. Organisms include plants and animals.

The levels of organisation in the human body can be seen in the diagrams. The example includes the cardiovascular system (also known as the circulatory system). This system is responsible for transporting substances around the body, including oxygen and nutrients.

The functions of plant organs

Key points

- Roots – take in water from the soil and provide anchorage.
- Xylem – carries water and mineral salts.
- Phloem – carries glucose.
- Leaf – where photosynthesis takes place.

Key words: xylem, mesophyll, photosynthesis, phloem, root, stem, leaf

Bump up your grade

Make sure you remember the difference between the functions of xylem and phloem. Try remembering that phloem starts with an 'f' sound as in food. The phloem carries dissolved food around the plant.

Plants are also organised into a number of levels.

Plant tissues

Specialised plant cells include root hair cells and xylem and phloem cells (for pictures of these cells see A.1 The basic structure, function and adaptations of cells). These cells group together to form tissues. Plant tissues include:

- **xylem** – carries water and mineral salts. It is made of dead cells with no end walls between the cells. It transports substances in one direction – from the roots to the stems and leaves.
- **mesophyll** – carries out **photosynthesis** to produce glucose.
- **phloem** – carries dissolved food, mainly the sugar glucose. Phloem is made of living cells that transport substances made in the leaves to growing regions, such as new shoots, and to storage organs in the plant. It transports substances in all directions.

> **1** *What process occurs in mesophyll tissue?*

Plant organs

Plant tissues group together to form organs. Plant organs include:

- **root** – absorbs water and mineral salts from the soil. It contains root hair cells that have a large surface area to speed up this process. Roots are also important for anchoring the plant into the ground so that it does not fall over.
- **stem** – supports the leaves and the flowers, keeping the plant upright. It also contains the xylem and phloem tissues, which transport substances between organs.
- **leaf** – this is the organ responsible for photosynthesis. Cells in the leaf contain large numbers of chloroplasts. The chloroplasts are full of a chemical known as chlorophyll. Chlorophyll absorbs sunlight and uses its energy to convert carbon dioxide and water into glucose and oxygen.

Photosynthesis can be summarised in the equation:

$$\text{carbon dioxide} + \text{water} \xrightarrow[\text{trapped in chlorophyll}]{\text{energy from sunlight}} \text{glucose} + \text{oxygen}$$

> **2** *Apart from taking in water, what is the other key function of the root?*

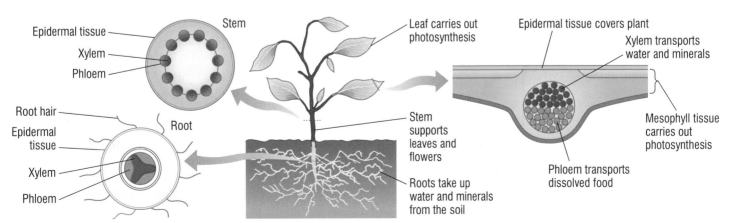

Plant organs and tissues

A.5

Transpiration

Water is constantly moving through a plant from the roots to the leaves through the xylem. This movement is called the **transpiration stream**.

The transpiration stream

Stomata on the surface of leaves can be opened and closed by guard cells (see A.1 The basic structure, function and adaptations of cells). Stomata open to allow carbon dioxide to enter the plant for photosynthesis. When they are open, water vapour is lost from the plant. Water evaporates from plant cells into the air spaces in leaves. It then diffuses out of the leaf through the stomata. This is called **transpiration**.

> **1 Through which structure does water leave a plant?**

Water is needed in a plant for photosynthesis and to prevent it from wilting, so it is important that the water is replaced. As the water evaporates from the leaf, more water is pulled up through the xylem to take its place. This results in a continuous flow of water from the roots to the leaves.

> **2 What does a plant need water for?**

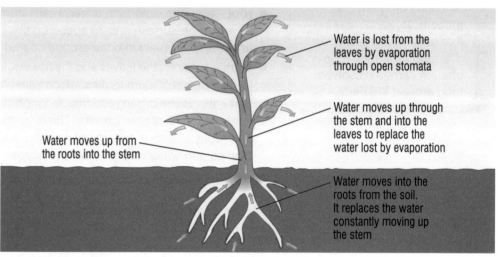

Water is lost from the leaves by evaporation through open stomata

Water moves up through the stem and into the leaves to replace the water lost by evaporation

Water moves up from the roots into the stem

Water moves into the roots from the soil. It replaces the water constantly moving up the stem

The transpiration stream

Factors affecting transpiration

More transpiration takes place during the day than during the night. This is when the stomata are open. The amount of transpiration which takes place is also affected by:
- wind – the more wind, the higher the transpiration rate
- humidity – the more humid the environment, the lower the transpiration rate
- temperature – the higher the temperature, the higher the transpiration rate.

> **3 Name four factors which affect the rate of transpiration.**

Key words: transpiration stream, stomata, transpiration

1 Name three types of animal cell.

2 What is the function of the nucleus of a cell?

3 Which plant organ does most photosynthesis occur in?

4 What are organ systems made up of?

5 What are the functions of the root?

6 Name two ways a sperm cell is adapted to its function.

7 Which components are found in both plant and animal cells?

8 What is the difference between a motor neurone and a sensory neurone?

9 Describe the levels of cellular organisation within an organism.

10 How do the xylem and phloem differ in their structures?

11 How is the transpiration stream maintained in a plant?

Checklist

Tick when you have:

reviewed it after your lesson ☑ ☐ ☐

revised once – some questions right ☑ ☑ ☐

revised twice – all questions right ☑ ☑ ☑

Move on to another topic when you have all three ticks

The basic structure, function and adaptations of cells ☐ ☐ ☐

The function of the components of cells ☐ ☐ ☐

Cells, tissues and organs ☐ ☐ ☐

The functions of plant organs ☐ ☐ ☐

Transpiration ☐ ☐ ☐

A.6

Key points

- DNA is a double helix.
- DNA contains a sequence of complementary base pairs.
- Adenine pairs with thymine.
- Guanine pairs with cytosine.

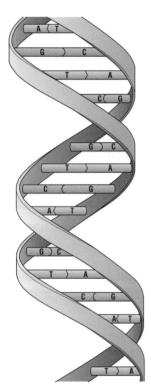

DNA – a double helix

DNA

What is DNA?

DNA stands for deoxyribonucleic acid. This is the chemical that contains all the genetic information required to make an organism. DNA is found in the nucleus of plant and animal cells.

Almost everyone's DNA is unique. The only organisms who share identical DNA are identical twins and **clones**.

▶ **1** *Where is DNA found in a plant or animal cell?*

Structure of DNA

DNA is a long molecule. It exists as two strands twisted together, and is called a double helix. It looks like a twisted ladder.

▶ **2** *Why is DNA called a double helix?*

Each strand of DNA is made up of chemicals called bases. There are four different types of bases – **adenine**, **thymine**, **guanine** and **cytosine**. These are often referred to by a single letter, as shown in the diagram. A = adenine, T = thymine, C = cytosine and G = guanine.

▶ **3** *Name the four bases found in DNA.*

In DNA, two strands coil together to form a double helix. They are held together by bonds formed between pairs of bases. The base pairs always bond together in the same formation – this is known as complementary base pairing:

- adenine always pairs with thymine
- cytosine always pairs with guanine.

Key words: DNA, clones, adenine, thymine, guanine, cytosine

Bump up your grade

Lots of exam questions require you to complete the genetic code in a section of DNA. They will give you the code for one strand and you have to write which bases pair with it. Remember AT and COG to help you – adenine pairs with thymine (AT) and cytosine pairs with guanine (COG).

A.7

Chromosomes and genes

Chromosomes

Chromosomes are long strands of DNA. They are found inside the nucleus of plant and animal cells. Each different type of organism has a different number of chromosomes in its nucleus. For example, humans have 46 chromosomes (23 pairs of chromosomes) but a fruit fly has only 8. You inherit half your chromosomes from your mother and half from your father.

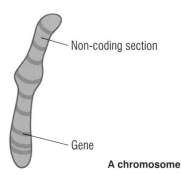

Non-coding section

Gene

A chromosome

Each chromosome is divided into sections of DNA. The sections of DNA that contain the information needed to produce a characteristic are called **genes**.

Genes

Genes contain the genetic information to code for a particular characteristic. However, when put together, genes control what the whole organism will look like. They determine its size, colour and shape. Genes also work at a molecular level coding for different proteins, including enzymes.

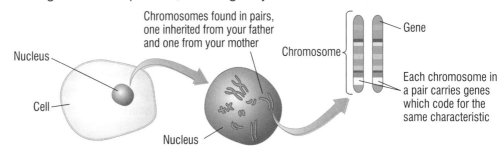

Chromosomes found in pairs, one inherited from your father and one from your mother

Nucleus

Cell

Nucleus

Gene

Chromosome

Each chromosome in a pair carries genes which code for the same characteristic

The nucleus contains the chromosomes that carry the genes which control the body's characteristics

A.8

Alleles

What are alleles?

For each characteristic a person has two genes, one from their mother and one from their father. These two genes may be the same, but they may be different. For example, one version of a gene could code for brown hair and one for black hair. Different forms of the same gene are called **alleles**.

When studying genetics, genes are normally represented using letters. For example, a gene could be represented by the letter A. The other allele would then be represented by the letter a.

- If an organism has two copies of an allele for a gene that are the same, it is called **homozygous**. For example, AA or aa.
- If an organism has two different copies of an allele for a gene, it is called **heterozygous**. For example, Aa.

Bump up your grade

To remember the difference between heterozygous and homozygous, think what the start of the word means. Hetero- means different and homo- means the same. For example, there is a man and a woman in a heterosexual relationship, and in a homosexual relationship the partners are of the same sex.

A.9

Exam tip

When you choose a letter to represent a genetic symbol, pick one that looks different in lowercase and uppercase, such as an A or an E. This makes it easy for the examiner to see which is uppercase, and which is lowercase. Letters such as C and c, or S and s, can be confusing.

Monohybrid inheritance

Dominant and recessive alleles

Some alleles will always be expressed if they are present in the nucleus. This means that the physical characteristic, which the allele codes for, will be present. These alleles are called **dominant alleles**. For example, the allele that codes for black hair is dominant. Therefore, if it is present inside your cells, you will have black hair. If the allele for blonde hair is also present in your cells, it will not be shown. This is because the black hair allele is stronger.

Weaker alleles like the blonde hair allele are called **recessive alleles**. Recessive alleles will only be expressed if you have two copies of them.

> 1 *Which type of allele will always be expressed if it is present?*

Studying inheritance

Scientists are able to predict what an organism's offspring will look like by carrying out genetic crosses. In the exam you may be asked to carry out genetic crosses to study the inheritance of one gene. This is called **monohybrid inheritance**.

When carrying out a genetic cross, the dominant allele is always represented with a capital letter. A lower case letter is used for the recessive allele. For example, when studying eye colour, brown eyes are dominant and blue eyes are recessive. If we chose the letter B to represent eye colour, B would represent the allele for brown eyes and b would represent the allele for blue eyes.

> 2 *Is a capital letter used to represent a dominant allele or a recessive allele?*

During fertilisation, one gene from the mother's egg joins with one gene from the father's sperm. This results in the combination of alleles present in the offspring. What happens during fertilisation can be represented on a **genetic diagram** or a **Punnett square**. These diagrams are used by scientists to predict characteristics.

> 3 *Name two types of diagram that can be used to represent genetic crosses.*

Genetic diagrams

In a genetic diagram, start by drawing the alleles each parent contains. There will be two alleles for each parent. You then draw criss-cross lines to show all the possible ways that these alleles could be paired in the offspring. There will be four possible ways, but some or all of the combinations of alleles may be repeated. Remember, if an organism only has one offspring, only one of these possibilities will actually happen.

Follow the genetic diagram below to see what happens when you cross a father with brown eyes (BB) and a mother with blue eyes (bb).

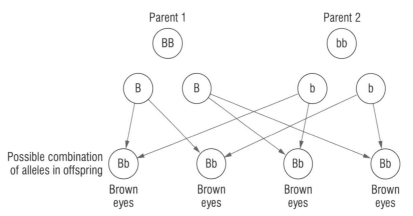

Genetic diagrams can be used to predict the characteristics of offspring

Punnett squares

Punnett squares are another technique scientists use to carry out genetic crosses. A Punnett square is used in the diagram below to show what happens when a mother with blue eyes (bb) is crossed with a father with brown eyes (BB). The result will be the same as in the first cross. This is a different way of showing what happens.

To produce a Punnett square, put the possible alleles from one parent across the top of the square (in this example the father has been placed across the top). Then put possible alleles from the other parent down the side. The pairs of letters show the possible combinations of alleles in the offspring.

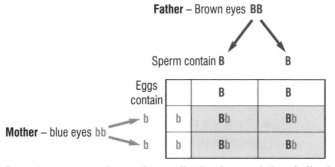

Punnett squares can be used to predict the characteristics of offspring

All children will have the genes Bb. This means that they will all have brown eyes, as B is the dominant allele. Remember – you have two genes for each characteristic.

> **4** *Why do all the children have brown eyes?*

> **Key words:** dominant allele, recessive allele, monohybrid inheritance, genetic diagram, Punnett square

A.10

- Pedigree analysis is used to work out the likelihood of a condition being inherited.
- Pedigree analysis studies a person's family tree.
- A carrier is a person who has a copy of a recessive allele but does not suffer from the disease.

Key words: pedigree analysis, genetically inherited disorder, carrier

Pedigree analysis

You can trace genetic characteristics through a family by drawing a family tree. Family trees show the males and females, and their characteristics. Doctors can use these diagrams to work out the likelihood that someone in a family will inherit a condition. This is called **pedigree analysis**.

Pedigree analysis

All the family members are mapped onto a family tree. Squares are used to represent males and circles to represent females. Those with and without a certain characteristic are then shown through shading.

▶ **1** *What shape in a pedigree analysis diagram is used to represent a female?*

In the diagram below the inheritance of dimples is shown. Pink shading represents those who have dimples and blue shading represents those without dimples.

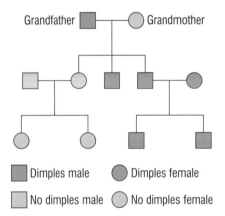

A pedigree analysis diagram showing the inheritance of dimples

We can tell a number of things from looking at this diagram:
- The allele coding for dimples must be dominant as when two parents with dimples reproduce all the offspring have dimples. We could represent this allele using D.
- The allele coding for no dimples must be recessive as it is only definitely expressed if both parents have no dimples. We could represent this allele using d.
- The grandmother must be homozygous for no dimples – dd. Otherwise she would have dimples.
- The grandfather must be heterozygous for dimples – Dd. He has dimples, so must have at least one dominant allele. However, he had a daughter with no dimples, therefore he must also carry the recessive allele. This would have joined with one of his wife's recessive alleles to have a daughter who is dd.

Cystic fibrosis

Doctors can use pedigree analysis to work out the chances of a person inheriting a **genetically inherited disorder**. Genetically inherited disorders are passed from parents to their offspring in their genes.

▶ **2** *What is a genetically inherited disorder?*

Cystic fibrosis is a genetically inherited disorder. Sufferers produce excessive levels of mucus, causing chest infections and difficulty absorbing food. There is no cure, so if the condition is present in a family, doctors may predict how likely it is for a couple to have a child with the disorder. The couple can then make an informed decision over whether or not to try for a baby.

Cystic fibrosis is caused by a recessive allele, so you need two copies of the allele to have the disorder. This is referred to as being homozygous recessive. If you are homozygous dominant you will be healthy, as you have two copies of the dominant healthy allele. If you are heterozygous for the condition, you have one copy of the healthy dominant allele and one copy of the disorder causing recessive allele. The (healthy) dominant gene will be expressed, which means you will be healthy. These people are known as **carriers** – they carry a copy of the allele, but do not have the disorder and will have no symptoms.

▶ **3** *What is a carrier?*

The diagram below shows the inheritance of cystic fibrosis in one family. Blue shading represents the individuals who have the disorder.

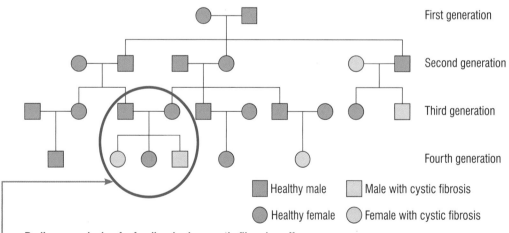

First generation

Second generation

Third generation

Fourth generation

■ Healthy male   ■ Male with cystic fibrosis
● Healthy female   ● Female with cystic fibrosis

Pedigree analysis of a family who has cystic fibrosis sufferers

If you knew nothing about cystic fibrosis you could work out a number of things from looking at this diagram:

- Cystic fibrosis must be caused by a recessive allele. In the third generation, two healthy individuals have produced children with cystic fibrosis. This means they must be carriers of the disorder. They must have one dominant healthy allele and one cystic fibrosis-causing recessive allele.
- People can be carriers of cystic fibrosis.
- As most people are healthy but there are some sufferers of the disorder, the healthy allele must be dominant. If the cystic fibrosis allele was dominant, there would be more sufferers than healthy people.

A.11

- A genotype is the genetic makeup of an individual.
- A phenotype describes the physical appearance of an individual.

Genotypes and phenotypes

Genotypes

A **genotype** tells you the genetic makeup of an individual – it tells you which alleles are present in the organism. An organism can be heterozygous for a characteristic, homozygous dominant or homozygous recessive.

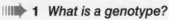 **1 What is a genotype?**

Phenotypes

A **phenotype** tells you what an organism actually looks like – it does not tell you which alleles are present. Therefore, you cannot tell if an organism is a carrier for a condition.

➡ **2 What is a phenotype?**

Tall pea plants are dominant (represented by T) to dwarf pea plants (represented by t). The table shows you the different genotypes and phenotypes an organism could have:

Genotype	Phenotype
TT	Tall
Tt	Tall
tt	Dwarf

Determining phenotypes and genotypes from genetic diagrams

In the diagram below red flowers are crossed with white flowers. The allele for red flowers (represented by F) is dominant to white flowers (represented by f). Use the genetic diagram to work out the phenotype and genotype of the offspring.

Bump up your grade

There are lots of technical terms used in genetics – you need to be certain you understand what is meant by each term. Try using the glossary to make your own genetics mini-dictionary to help you learn them.

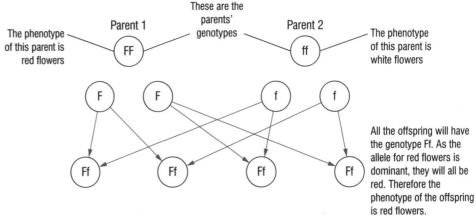

Genetic cross between red and white flowers

Determining phenotypes and genotypes from pedigree analysis

Look at the diagram below showing the inheritance of ginger hair. The allele for ginger hair is recessive (represented by h). Can you work out the phenotype and genotype of Sue, Louise and Kevin?

You should use the key to work out the phenotype first. Then use your knowledge of inheritance to work out the genotype of each person.

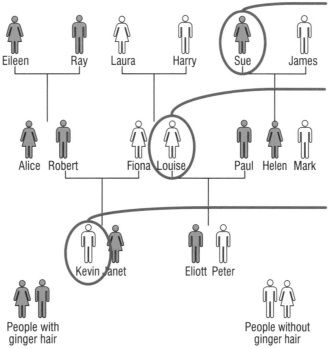

Sue: Phenotype – ginger hair
        Genotype – hh

Ginger hair is recessive. Sue must have two copies of this allele for it to be expressed.

Louise: Phenotype – not ginger hair
        Genotype – Hh

Louise has to be heterozygous for the condition in order to have a son (Eliott) with ginger hair. Eliott must have two recessive alleles as he has ginger hair, one from his mother and one from his father.

Kevin: Phenotype – not ginger hair
         Genotype – Hh

Kevin whould inherit a recessive allele from his father and a dominant allele from his mother. Ginger hair is recessive, so Kevin will not have ginger hair.

People with ginger hair

People without ginger hair

Inheritance of ginger hair

Key words: genotype, phenotype

Bump up your grade

You may find it helpful to use two different colour pens when drawing genetic crosses. Use one colour to represent the mother's gene and the other to represent the father's gene. You can then check that each offspring contains one gene from its mother and one from its father.

A.12

Calculating the likelihood of offspring displaying a particular characteristic

When studying genetic crosses, it is possible to calculate the possibility of an offspring displaying a particular characteristic. This can be stated in one of three ways – as a probability, as a percentage, or as a ratio.

 Maths skills – Probability, ratio and percentages

Probabilities, ratio and percentages can all be used to describe outcomes. They tell you how likely something is to occur.

Imagine you have completed a survey of eye colour in your class. 10 students have brown eyes and 5 students have blue eyes.

● Percentages are a proportion, expressed out of 100%. In this class, 10 out of 15 students are brown-eyed. This is calculated as $\frac{10}{15} \times 100 = 67\%$ with brown eyes.

● Ratios compare amounts – they are always expressed as one amount compared to another. In this class, 10 students have brown eyes and 5 have blue eyes. There are 2 brown-eyed students to every 1 blue-eyed student. This is written as the ratio 10:5, which can be simplified to 2:1.

● Probability is the chance of an event occurring, expressed as a '1 in X chance'. In this class, there is a 10 in 15 chance (or, simplified, a 2 in 3 chance) of a student having brown eyes.

The table below shows the ones you are most likely to come across:

Probability (chance)	Ratio	Percentage
4 in 4	4:0	100%
3 in 4	3:1	75%
2 in 4 (simplifies to 1 in 2)	2:2 (simplifies to 1:1)	50%
1 in 4	1:3	25%
0 in 4	0:4	0%

▻ 1 *How would you express 75% as a ratio?*

▻ 2 *How would you express 25% as a probability?*

Sickle-cell anaemia

Sickle-cell anaemia is a genetically inherited disorder. Sufferers have sickle-shaped red blood cells that stop them carrying oxygen properly. It is caused by a recessive allele (represented by a). Use the diagram at the top of the next page to calculate the likelihood of two **carriers** of sickle-cell anaemia having a child with the disorder.

▻ 3 *What alleles do you have if you are a carrier of sickle-cell anaemia?*

BOOK ORDER (3)

HARROW COLLEGE LEARNING CENTRE 38240.001-002

Supplier	Dawson Books (UK)	Order Ref	FORD25725W
Order Date	29/08/2013	Item Ref	13SCI
Quantity	2	ISBN	9781408518427
Unit Price	5.99	Currency	GBP
Instructions			

Author	Locke, Jo		
Title	BTEC FIRST APPLIED SCIENCE PRINCIPLES OF APPLIED SCIENCE UNIT 1 REVISION GUIDE		
Volume		Edition	NEW EDITION
Format		Publisher	NELSON THORNES
Shelf Mark		Date Publ.	10/09/2012
Site	HW		
Fund	13SCI		
Sequence			
Loan Type	STANDARD LOAN		
Quantity	2		

Dawson Ref 5082855-006

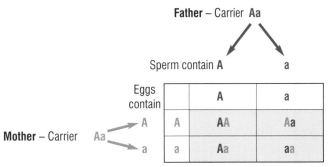

Inheritance of sickle-cell anaemia

These children will be carriers of the disorder, but they will be healthy and not suffer from it.

Offspring genotype   1AA : 2Aa : 1aa

Offspring phenotype   3 normal children : 1 sickle-cell anaemia sufferer

There is a 25% chance that their child will suffer from sickle-cell anaemia. This could also be stated as a 1 in 4 chance of having a child who suffers from the disorder.

Polydactyly

Polydactyly is a genetically inherited disorder where children are born with extra digits – fingers or toes. It is caused by a dominant allele (represented by D). Therefore people only need one copy of this allele to have the disorder. You cannot be a carrier of polydactyly.

4 Why can't you be a carrier of polydactyly?

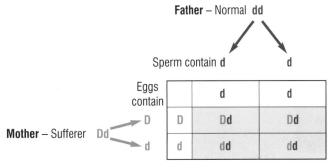

Inheritance of polydactyly

As polydactyly is caused by a dominant allele, these children will not be carriers. They will have the disorder.

Offspring genotype   2Dd : 2dd

Offspring phenotype   2 polydactyly sufferers : 2 normal children

There is a 50% chance that the child will suffer from polydactyly. This could also be stated as a 1 in 2 chance of having a child who suffers from the disorder.

Key word: carrier

A.13

- A genetic mutation occurs when there is a change in an organism's DNA.
- Genetic mutations can change an organism's characteristics.
- Genetic mutations can be harmful or beneficial to an organism.

Gene mutations

What are mutations?

Genetic **mutations** are changes that can occur to an organism's DNA. If the base sequence is altered within a coding section of the DNA (a **gene**) this can change the characteristic of an organism. Usually these changes are harmful, but occasionally they are beneficial.

 1 *What is a mutation?*

Mutations can happen spontaneously. Where they occur is due to chance. However, exposure to radiation and some chemicals increases the chance of mutations occurring. For example, the chemicals in cigarette smoke increase the risk of mutations in the lungs.

Harmful mutations

Most of the time, mutations cause no effect. Normally, the change in the DNA sequence occurs in part of the DNA that doesn't actually code for a protein, so it doesn't change anything about the organism. Even if the mutation does occur within a gene (a region of DNA that codes for a protein), it still may not alter the protein's structure, or cause a change in the function of the protein.

Sometimes these changes can be so severe that the cell dies. Occasionally mutations cause the body cells to reproduce uncontrollably. This can cause cancer.

 2 *Name a disease that can be caused by mutations.*

Beneficial mutations

Occasionally, mutations can cause beneficial changes resulting in new and useful characteristics. As these changes usually occur in normal body cells, the changes are lost when an organism dies. However, if the changes occur in sex cells (such as a sperm and an egg), they can be passed on to the next generation.

 3 *In what type of cell must a mutation occur if it is to be passed on to the next generation?*

Key words: mutation, gene

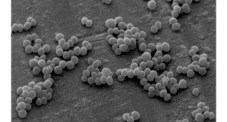

MRSA – these antibiotic-resistant bacteria have evolved as a result of a beneficial mutation. The mutation in their DNA increased their chance of survival by stopping certain antibiotics from killing them.

1 Where is DNA found in your body?

2 What is meant by a dominant allele?

3 Rearrange these structures in order of size, starting with the smallest:

cell, gene, nucleus, chromosome, a section of DNA.

4 What happens when a gene is mutated?

5 What is the difference between homozygous and heterozygous?

6 Write the complementary base sequence for this strand of DNA: ATTCGTACAG

7 Freckles are dominant to no freckles. If an organism has the following genotype, what is their phenotype?

a FF   **b** ff   **c** Ff

8 Cystic fibrosis is a genetically inherited disorder caused by a recessive allele. It is represented by the letter 'c'.

   a What is meant by a 'carrier of cystic fibrosis'?

   b Use a genetic diagram to determine the likelihood of a child having cystic fibrosis if two carrier parents are crossed. Express your answer as a ratio.

9 Polydactyly is a genetically inherited disorder caused by a dominant allele. It is represented by the letter D.

   a Draw a Punnett square if both parents are heterozygous for the disorder.

   b What percentage of offspring are likely to suffer from the disorder?

   c What is the phenotype of the parents?

Checklist ✓✓✓

Tick when you have:							
reviewed it after your lesson	✓	☐	☐	DNA	☐	☐	☐
revised once – some questions right	✓	✓	☐	Chromosomes and genes	☐	☐	☐
revised twice – all questions right	✓	✓	✓	Alleles	☐	☐	☐
Move on to another topic when you have all three ticks				Monohybrid inheritance	☐	☐	☐
				Pedigree analysis	☐	☐	☐
				Genotypes and phenotypes	☐	☐	☐
				Calculating the likelihood of offspring displaying a particular characteristic	☐	☐	☐
				Gene mutations	☐	☐	☐

1 The diagram here shows a typical animal cell:

  a **i** What substance is found in part A? *(1 mark)*

    ii Name the process that takes place inside the mitochondria. *(1 mark)*

    iii State **two** functions of part B. *(2 marks)*

  b **i** Why does an animal cell not have chloroplasts? *(1 mark)*

    ii As well as chloroplasts, plant cells have **two** additional structures. Name these **two** features. *(2 marks)*

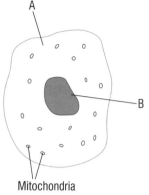

Mitochondria

Exam tip

Practise sketching a typical plant cell and animal cell. It is common for exam questions to ask you to identify the components in a cell.

2 Some cells are adapted like the ones below:

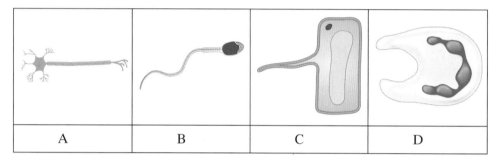

A	B	C	D

  a **i** Explain what is meant by an adapted cell. *(1 mark)*

    ii Identify cells A to D in the table. *(4 marks)*

  b **i** What is the function of a red blood cell? *(1 mark)*

    ii Explain how a red blood cell is adapted to perform its function. *(2 marks)*

3 The picture below shows the movement of water through a plant:

  a **i** What is the name given to the movement of water through a plant? *(1 mark)*

    ii Name the cell through which water enters a plant. *(1 mark)*

    iii Explain how this cell is adapted to take in water. *(3 marks)*

  b **i** Describe how water is moved through a plant from the roots to the leaves. *(2 marks)*

    ii State and explain **one** factor that increases the rate of transpiration. *(2 marks)*

Exam tip

Question 3bii is worth two marks. The question asks you to state *and* explain **one** factor that increases the rate of transpiration. One mark will be awarded for stating the factor. The other mark will be awarded for explaining how this increases the rate of transpiration.

4 Organisms are made up of different layers of organisation.

a i Complete the following table by adding **one** tick in each row to identify whether the structures are cells or organs. *(3 marks)*

Structure	Cell	Organ
Kidney		
Sperm		
Liver		

ii What is meant by a tissue? *(1 mark)*

b Explain how an organism is organised into levels of organisation, using the cardiovascular system to illustrate your answer. *(6 marks)*

5 Humans can be classified into those that have unattached ear lobes (not attached to their face) or those that have attached ear lobes. Attached ear lobes are an example of an inherited characteristic. Use the pedigree analysis diagram below to answer the following questions:

Pedigree for attached earlobes

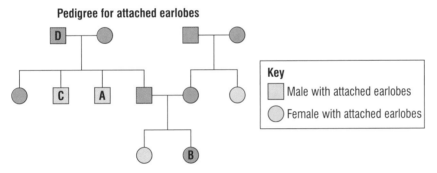

Key

☐ Male with attached earlobes

◯ Female with attached earlobes

a i What is the phenotype of person A? *(1 mark)*

ii What is the phenotype of person B? *(1 mark)*

b i Are attached ear lobes a dominant or recessive characteristic? Explain your answer. *(3 marks)*

ii What is the genotype of person C? *(1 mark)*

iii What is the genotype of person D? Explain your answer. *(3 marks)*

6 Tay Sachs disease is a fatal disorder in children that causes a degeneration of the central nervous system. It is a genetically inherited disorder caused by a recessive allele (t is normally used to represent this recessive allele).

a i What is meant by the term 'carrier'? *(2 marks)*

ii What would be the genotype of a carrier of Tay Sachs disease? *(1 mark)*

b i A man and a woman wish to have a child but know there have been some cases of Tay Sachs disease in previous generations of their family. Draw out a genetic cross or Punnett square to show the possible genotypes of their offspring. Assume both parents are heterozygous for the condition. *(2 marks)*

ii What is the probability of them having a child suffering from Tay Sachs disease? *(1 mark)*

iii Calculate the percentage of their offspring that will be carriers of Tay Sachs disease. *(1 mark)*

Exam tip

All the information you need to answer question 5 is contained in the pedigree analysis chart. The question is not testing you on your knowledge of the inheritance of earlobes, but on your understanding of these charts.

Begin with the grandparents and work slowly through the offspring. If a characteristic is present in the children that neither of the parents displayed, it must be a recessive characteristic.

Exam tip

There are two different ways of calculating the likelihood of a genetic condition being inherited – Punnett squares and genetic crosses. Whichever method you choose to use, ensure you make your working very clear to the examiner.

B.1

Homeostasis

Hormones

Hormones are chemical messengers that travel around your body. They are made in **glands** and secreted into the blood. The blood transports the hormones around the body. Hormones cause a response in specific cells found in target organs. For example, testosterone is produced in the testes and causes sperm production.

> ### Exam tip
>
> Some hormones have multiple target organs. For example, adrenaline is produced by the adrenal glands and targets many organs, including the liver and heart. It prepares the body for action in the 'fight or flight' response (see B.5 Reflexes).

 1 *How do hormones travel around the body?*

Nerves

Nerves transmit electrical impulses around the body. Nerves detect changes in an organism's environment and usually send impulses to the brain. The brain processes this information and decides on an appropriate response. It then sends an impulse to another part of the body, telling it what to do.

 2 *What do nerves do?*

Homeostasis

In order to function normally, it is essential that the body's internal environment is kept constant. This maintenance of a constant internal environment is called **homeostasis**. Many internal systems have to be controlled. These include:

- body temperature – this is controlled by changes in the skin
- blood glucose concentration – this is controlled by hormones in the liver and the pancreas
- water concentration – this is controlled by the kidneys.

 3 *What is meant by the term 'homeostasis'?*

Key words: hormones, glands, nerves, homeostasis

B.2

Key points

- The nervous system consists of the central nervous system (CNS) and the peripheral nervous system (PNS).
- The CNS is made up of the brain and spinal cord.
- The PNS is made up of the sensory and motor neurones.

Structure of the nervous system

The nervous system controls the actions of your body. It coordinates different parts of the body so that they all work together. For example, it coordinates all the muscles in your legs so that you can walk. It also coordinates things you don't think about, such as breathing and swallowing.

The nervous system is divided into two main parts – the central nervous system and the peripheral nervous system.

Central nervous system

The **central nervous system**, normally referred to as the CNS, consists of the brain and the spinal cord. These structures are made of delicate nervous tissue, so they are protected by bones. The skull protects the brain and the vertebral column (backbone) protects the spine.

The CNS receives information about changes in the body's environment and decides how to respond.

> **1** *Which two structures make up the central nervous system?*

Peripheral nervous system

The **peripheral nervous system**, normally referred to as the PNS, consists of **sensory neurones** and **motor neurones**. The PNS transmits electrical impulses containing information to and from the CNS:

- sensory neurones – carry impulses containing information about changes in the external environment into the CNS
- motor neurones – carry impulses containing information about how the body should respond from the CNS to muscles or glands.

> **2** *Which two structures make up the peripheral nervous system?*

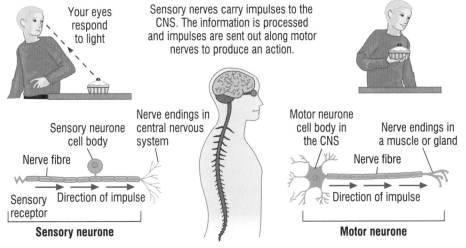

The rapid responses of our nervous system allow us to respond to our surroundings very quickly

Key words: central nervous system (CNS), peripheral nervous system (PNS), sensory neurone, motor neurone

Exam tip

Many people may think that nerve cells are long and thin so that they can 'travel' through the body more easily. Nerve cells do not 'travel', but they do stretch over long distances, for example, from your big toe to the spinal cord.

B.3

Voluntary and involuntary responses

There are two main types of nervous action the body carries out – **voluntary responses** and **involuntary responses**.

Voluntary responses

Voluntary responses (or voluntary actions) occur as a result of you consciously deciding you want to do something. For example, if you see a friend in the distance you may wish to attract their attention, so you wave and call out their name. This is a voluntary response – your brain sends impulses to the muscles of your arm, causing your arm to wave. It also sends impulses to your larynx, causing you to call to your friend.

▶ **1** *What is a voluntary response?*

Involuntary responses

Involuntary responses or (involuntary actions) occur without you thinking. Your spinal cord or your brain takes total control of the action without you consciously thinking. Examples of involuntary responses include blinking, sneezing and your heart beating.

▶ **2** *What is an involuntary response?*

B.4

Transmission of electrical impulses along neurones and chemical transmission across synapses

Stages of a nervous response

There are three stages to a nervous response:
1 **stimulus** – a change in the environment
2 **receptors** – groups of cells that detect the stimulus
3 **effectors** – they cause a response (muscles or glands).

Receptors

Receptors are groups of cells found in your sense organs, such as your eyes and ears. Receptor cells detect stimuli such as light, heat and sound. They change the stimulus into electrical impulses. These impulses travel along sensory neurones into the central nervous system. Electrical impulses travel very quickly – up to 120 metres every second!

▶ **1** *What is a receptor?*

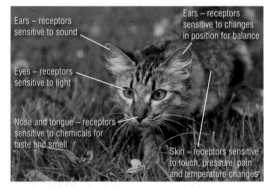

Ears – receptors sensitive to sound

Ears – receptors sensitive to changes in position for balance

Eyes – receptors sensitive to light

Nose and tongue – receptors sensitive to chemicals for taste and smell

Skin – receptors sensitive to touch, pressure, pain and temperature changes

This cat relies on receptor cells in its sensory organs to detect changes in the environment

Effectors

Your brain receives large amounts of information from all the sensory receptors in your body. The brain coordinates this information then sends electrical impulses along motor neurones to the effectors. The effectors are muscles or glands. They bring about the changes required. Muscles respond to the impulse by contracting. This causes movement. Glands respond by releasing hormones.

2 What is an effector?

The steps in a voluntary nervous response are shown in the flow diagram below:

stimulus → receptor → sensory neurone → spinal cord → brain → spinal cord → motor neurone → effector → response

How do impulses travel along neurones?

The long projection from a neurone cell is called an axon. Electrical impulses travel along the axon.

The sheath surrounding the axon is made of fat. This acts as an insulator – like the plastic coating surrounding a wire. The sheath makes the impulse travel faster and it prevents the information being scrambled.

Neurones also have branched endings at either end of the cell. These allow the neurone to connect with many other neurones.

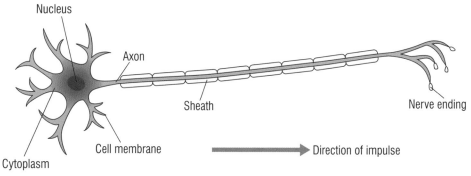

Nucleus

Axon

Sheath

Nerve ending

Cell membrane

Cytoplasm

Direction of impulse

Structure of a motor neurone

3 How does a nerve cell transmit information?

How does information pass between neurones?

Impulse arrives in neurone

Sacs containing chemicals

Receptor site

Chemicals are released into the gap between neurones

Chemicals attach to the surface of the next neurone and set up a new electrical impulse

Chemical transmission across a synapse

Your neurones are not connected directly to each other. There are gaps between them called **synapses**. The electrical impulses travelling along your neurones have to cross these gaps, but they cannot jump. When an impulse arrives at a synapse, chemicals are released which diffuse across the synapse. When they arrive at the next neurone the chemicals bind to receptor sites. This triggers an electrical impulse in the next neurone.

Only one end of a neurone can make the chemical – this ensures that the impulse can travel in only one direction.

4 How does the impulse travel from one neurone to the next?

B.5

Reflexes

Reflex actions are automatic responses to a stimulus. They occur without thinking and do not involve the brain. As they miss out the brain, the body can react even more quickly. The body uses these reactions when we are in danger.

The steps in a reflex response are shown in the flow diagram below:

stimulus → receptor → sensory neurone → spinal cord → motor neurone → effector → response

▐▶ **1** *How does a reflex action differ from a voluntary nervous response?*

Examples of reflex actions

The table shows a range of situations where a person is in potential danger. The body's reflex actions occur rapidly to prevent the person getting hurt.

Potential danger	Reflex action
Bright sunshine could damage the retina.	Muscles in the iris contract, making the pupil smaller. This prevents light damaging the retina.
Choking on an object.	Muscles at the back of the throat contract, preventing the object from entering.
Cutting your hand on broken glass.	Biceps contract, pulling your arm away from the glass.
Sand blowing into your eyes.	Muscles contract, causing blinking. This prevents sand entering your eyes.
Interaction with someone who threatens you.	Adrenaline is released. This prepares the body for rapid activity by increasing the heart rate and blood glucose concentration. This is known as the 'fight or flight' response.

▐▶ **2** *Name two situations where a reflex action could prevent you from danger.*

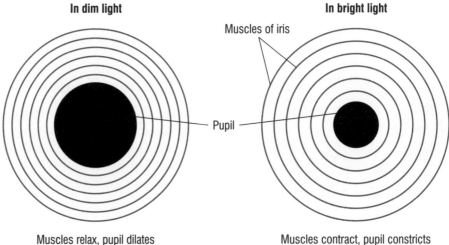

In dim light

In bright light

Muscles of iris

Pupil

Muscles relax, pupil dilates

Muscles contract, pupil constricts

The iris muscles control the diameter of the pupil

Reflex arc

The pathway that the impulse follows, from the receptor to the effector, during a reflex action is known as a **reflex arc**. The diagram below shows the reflex arc for the reflex action that occurs to prevent you burning your hand on a boiling hot saucepan.

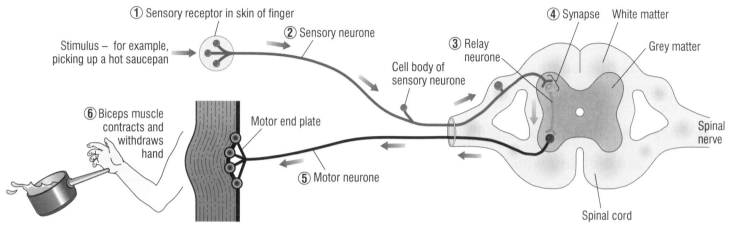

Reflex actions are quick and automatic. This action saves you from being badly burned.

1 Your hand touching the hot saucepan is detected by the temperature receptors in your skin.
2 An electrical impulse is triggered that travels along the sensory neurone to the CNS.
3 In the spinal cord, the impulse is passed onto a **relay neurone**. (Remember this occurs by chemicals being transmitted across the synapse.) Relay neurones connect sensory and motor neurones. They are only found in the CNS.
4 The relay neurone then releases chemicals to transmit the impulse across the synapse to the motor neurone.
5 The motor neurone transmits the impulse to the biceps muscle.
6 The biceps muscle is an effector and it contracts. This moves your hand away from the saucepan.

Key words: reflex action, reflex arc, relay neurone

▶ **3** *What do relay neurones do?*

> ### Exam tip
>
> If you are asked to describe a reflex arc it is often easier to draw a flow diagram. Start by writing out the standard flow diagram and then add sentences to make it specific to the reaction you are describing. The reflex action for stopping your hand being burnt on a hot saucepan could be explained like this:
>
> Stimulus – very hot saucepan
> ↓
> Receptor – temperature receptors in skin
> ↓
> Sensory neurone
> ↓
> Spinal cord
> ↓
> Motor neurone
> ↓
> Effector – biceps muscle contracts
> ↓
> Response – hand pulled away

1 What is the role of a hormone in the body?

2 What is the difference between the CNS and the PNS?

3 What is the difference between a voluntary and an involuntary response?

4 What is homeostasis? Name two factors which must be maintained by homeostasis.

5 Are the following reactions voluntary or reflex actions?

   a Eyes blinking when the wind blows on the beach.

   b Answering a question.

   c Texting a friend.

   d Sneezing when dust goes up your nose.

6 Describe how impulses are transmitted across synapses.

7 Explain how a neurone is adapted to its function in transmitting impulses.

8 Explain why reflex actions occur more quickly than voluntary responses. Why is this important?

9 Describe the reflex arc that takes place when your toe is stung by a bee.

Checklist ✓ ✓ ✓

Tick when you have:				Homeostasis	☐ ☐ ☐
reviewed it after your lesson	☑ ☐ ☐			Structure of the nervous system	☐ ☐ ☐
revised once – some questions right	☑ ☑ ☐			Voluntary and involuntary responses	☐ ☐ ☐
revised twice – all questions right	☑ ☑ ☑			Transmission of electrical impulses along neurones and chemical transmission across synapses	☐ ☐ ☐
Move on to another topic when you have all three ticks				Reflexes	☐ ☐ ☐

B.6

The endocrine system

The endocrine system is made up of glands that release hormones. Together with the nervous system, the endocrine system controls and coordinates body processes.

Hormones

Hormones are chemical substances that coordinate many body processes. **Glands** make hormones and release (secrete) them into the blood. The hormones are then carried around the body in the bloodstream to other parts of the body. Hormones cause a response in specific cells found in **target organs**.

⟹ 1 *Where are hormones produced?*

⟹ 2 *Where do hormones cause an effect?*

Hormones regulate the functions of many cells and organs. They can act fairly quickly, for example, when adrenaline is released. However, they can only travel at the speed at which your blood moves. Normally, hormonal responses are fairly slow and long lasting. For example, oestrogen and testosterone are responsible for changes which take place during puberty.

⟹ 3 *How quickly can hormones travel around the body?*

Sites of hormone production

The diagram below shows the position of some important glands and the hormones they produce:

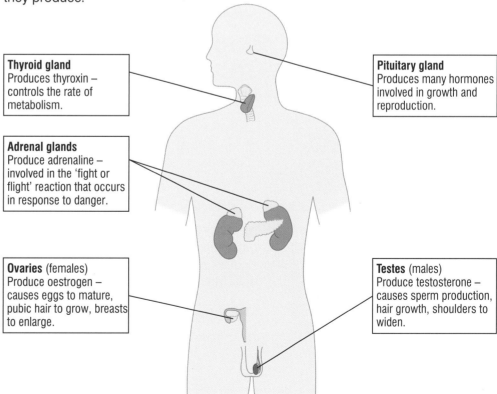

Thyroid gland
Produces thyroxin – controls the rate of metabolism.

Pituitary gland
Produces many hormones involved in growth and reproduction.

Adrenal glands
Produce adrenaline – involved in the 'fight or flight' reaction that occurs in response to danger.

Ovaries (females)
Produce oestrogen – causes eggs to mature, pubic hair to grow, breasts to enlarge.

Testes (males)
Produce testosterone – causes sperm production, hair growth, shoulders to widen.

Position of glands in the body

B.7

The endocrine and nervous system

The endocrine system and nervous system both carry out similar roles. Using **hormones** and **nerves**, they send messages around the body to provide information about any changes that are taking place in both the internal and external environment. They also send information as to how the body should respond to any changes.

However, nerves and hormones carry out their roles in very different ways. The table below summarises these differences:

	Nerves	**Hormones**
Speed of communication	Very fast	Slower
Method of transport/transmission	Electrical impulse along the axon	In the blood
Duration of response	Short acting	Long acting
Area targeted	Very precise area	Large area

1 *Do nerves or hormones produce a more rapid response?*

2 *How do nerves and hormones differ in the duration of their response?*

Key words: hormones, nerves

B.8

Blood glucose concentration

Glucose (a type of sugar) is used in respiration to release energy. To remain healthy it is important that the concentration of glucose in your blood is kept constant. Without control, your blood glucose concentration would range from very high after a meal to very low several hours later – so low that cells would not have enough glucose for respiration. Two hormones, **insulin** and **glucagon**, ensure that your blood glucose concentration remains constant.

Increasing blood glucose concentration

When you eat carbohydrate-rich foods, such as pasta and rice, they are broken down in the digestive system to release glucose. Sweet foods, such as cakes and chocolate, also contain high levels of sugar. The glucose released by digestion passes into the blood and causes the blood glucose concentration to rise.

1 *How does glucose enter the body?*

Decreasing blood glucose concentration

Some of the glucose in the blood is used by cells to release energy. This is required to perform normal body functions. If you exercise, more glucose will be needed as the body needs to generate more energy. Any extra glucose in the blood is stored in the liver until it is needed.

Insulin

Insulin is a hormone produced by the pancreas. If the blood glucose concentration is too high, insulin is released. Insulin makes the liver remove glucose from the blood. It does this by turning glucose into **glycogen** – a store of energy. Glycogen is then stored in the liver. As there is now less glucose in the blood, the blood glucose concentration falls.

⟱➤ **2 Where is insulin made?**

⟱➤ **3 What is glycogen?**

Glucagon

Glucagon is also produced by the pancreas. If the blood glucose concentration is too low, the pancreas releases glucagon. Glucagon makes the liver change glycogen back into glucose. This is then released into the blood, causing the blood glucose concentration to rise.

⟱➤ **4 Which hormone increases the blood glucose concentration?**

The flow diagram below shows how insulin and glucagon work together to maintain a constant blood glucose concentration:

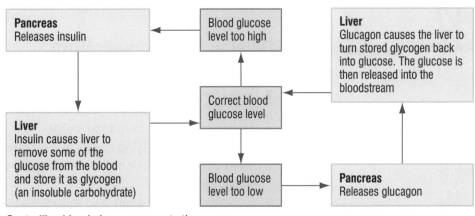

Controlling blood glucose concentration

Key words: insulin, glucagon, glycogen

B.9

Key points

- The brain monitors and regulates body temperature using the nervous system.
- Your body increases its body temperature through shivering and the hairs on your skin standing up.
- Your body lowers its body temperature by sweating and lowering the hairs on the skin so they lie flat.
- Vasodilation is when the blood vessels supplying the skin capillaries widen.
- Vasoconstriction is when the blood vessels supplying the skin capillaries narrow.

Key words: homeostasis, sweat, vasodilation, vasoconstriction, shiver

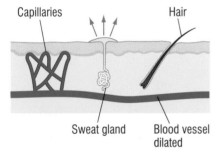

Capillaries — Hair

Sweat gland — Blood vessel dilated

Skin's appearance when a person is hot

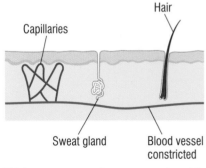

Hair

Capillaries

Sweat gland — Blood vessel constricted

Skin's appearance when a person is cold

Maintaining body temperature

Monitoring body temperature

The thermoregulatory centre in the brain is responsible for regulating body temperature. It contains receptors that monitor the blood's temperature. Temperature receptors in the skin also send information to the brain about the skin's temperature. When a change in body temperature is detected, the brain causes different parts of the body to respond. These responses should return the body back to its normal temperature. This is an example of **homeostasis** (the maintenance of a constant internal environment, see B.1 Homeostasis).

The body must remain at 37 °C. A couple of degrees change in either direction stops the body working efficiently. For example, if a person is too hot, they may suffer from dehydration. If they are too cold, their body movements will slow and could eventually result in death.

▶ **1** *What is normal body temperature?*

Lowering body temperature

If you get too hot, your body does a number of things to lower your temperature:

- Body hairs are lowered so the hairs on your skin lie flat. This prevents an insulating layer of air being trapped around the body.
- Sweat glands produce **sweat**. Sweat is mainly made of water. As the water in sweat evaporates from your body, you lose heat energy. This reduces your body temperature.
- Blood vessels supplying capillaries near the surface of your skin widen. This is known as **vasodilation**. This increases the blood flow through the capillaries, which increases heat loss by radiation.

▶ **2** *How does sweat cool you down?*

Raising body temperature

If you get too cold, your body does a number of things to raise your temperature:

- Body hairs rise – the hairs on your skin stand on end, trapping a layer of air close to the skin. This insulates the body, which reduces heat loss.
- Sweat glands do not produce sweat.
- Blood vessels supplying capillaries near the surface of your skin narrow. This is called **vasoconstriction**. This reduces the blood flow through the capillaries, which reduces heat loss.
- You **shiver** – this is when your muscles contract quickly. This requires extra energy, so your cells respire more, producing extra heat.

▶ **3** *How does shivering raise your body temperature?*

Exam tip

If you are asked a question about maintaining body temperature, use the appearance of your own skin to help you. Are you feeling hot or cold – what does your skin look like? How does your skin's appearance change when you exercise?

1 How do hormones reach their target organs?

2 What does the body use glucose for?

3 What is glycogen?

4 Name three changes in the body that occur when a person gets too hot.

5 How does sweating cool you down?

6 What is the difference between vasodilation and vasoconstriction?

7 Describe the differences between a hormonal response and a nervous response.

8 **a** How does the brain monitor body temperature?

  b Why is this important?

9 **a** Explain how insulin controls blood glucose concentration.

  b Explain how glucagon controls blood glucose levels.

Checklist		✓	✓	✓
Tick when you have:				
reviewed it after your lesson	✓ ☐ ☐	The endocrine system	☐	☐	☐
revised once – some questions right	✓ ✓ ☐	The endocrine and nervous system	☐	☐	☐
revised twice – all questions right	✓ ✓ ✓	Blood glucose concentration	☐	☐	☐
Move on to another topic when you have all three ticks		Maintaining body temperature	☐	☐	☐

1 This picture shows a person's skin when they are cold.

Use the picture to help you describe what happens to each of the following structures in the skin when you are cold:

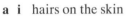

a i hairs on the skin   *(1 mark)*

   ii sweat glands   *(1 mark)*

   iii blood capillaries.   *(1 mark)*

b State and explain another mechanism your body has to warm you up when you are cold.   *(3 marks)*

2 Nerves and hormones both transmit messages around the body.

a Complete the table below, which compares how nerves and hormones operate. Some of the answers have been filled in for you.   *(3 marks)*

	Nerves	**Hormones**
Speed of communication	Very fast	
Method of transport/transmission		In the blood
Duration of response	Short	

b Complete the sentences below, by choosing appropriate words to describe what happens in a hormonal response.

Hormones are .... messengers produced in ....

The hormones are released into the blood, where they travel to ....   *(3 marks)*

c Name an example of a hormone.   *(1 mark)*

3 To remain healthy, the body's internal environment has to be kept constant.

a What is this process called?   *(1 mark)*

b Which **two** body systems work together to maintain a constant internal environment?   *(2 marks)*

c State and explain **one** factor in the body that must be kept constant.   *(2 marks)*

4 When we need to react quickly to danger, our body uses reflexes.

a State **one** reason why it is beneficial to uses reflexes, rather than a normal nervous response.   *(1 mark)*

b Complete the following table, to show if the following responses are reflex responses or voluntary responses. Place **one** tick in each row.

Activity	Voluntary response	Involuntary response
Pupils in your eyes contract in bright light		
Kick a ball		
Sign your name		
Removing your hand from a hot saucepan		

(2 marks)

c i What is the name of the neurone labelled C in the reflex arc? *(1 mark)*

ii Which neurone in the diagram is found solely within the central nervous system (CNS)? *(1 mark)*

iii What is the effector in the reflex arc? *(1 mark)*

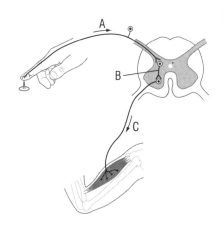

d Diabetics need to test their blood sugar levels regularly. How would the path the nervous impulse follows differ from a reflex arc if you made a conscious decision to prick yourself with a sharp object? *(1 mark)*

5 The graph below shows a person's blood glucose concentration throughout the day.

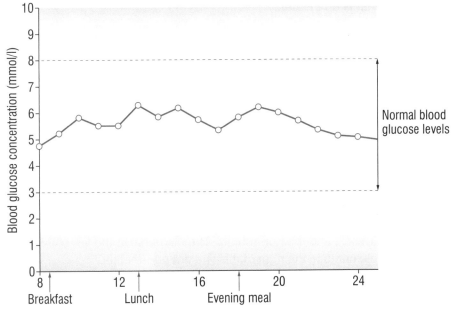

a i What is glucose used for in the body? *(1 mark)*

ii When do peaks in blood glucose concentration occur? *(1 mark)*

iii Explain why these peaks in blood glucose concentration occur. *(2 marks)*

b i Which hormone is responsible for reducing blood glucose concentration? *(1 mark)*

ii How does this hormone reduce blood glucose concentration? *(3 marks)*

c i Which hormone is responsible for increasing blood glucose concentration? *(1 mark)*

ii How does this hormone increase blood glucose concentration? *(3 marks)*

6 Your internal body temperature has to be constantly monitored to ensure it remains approximately constant. If your body temperature becomes too high, you can suffer dehydration. If you get too cold, you can fall into a coma.

a What is normal body temperature? *(1 mark)*

b i Which part of the brain is responsible for monitoring body temperature? *(1 mark)*

ii Explain how the brain regulates body temperature. *(3 marks)*

One of the changes that takes place in the skin is vasodilation.

c Explain the difference between vasodilation and vasoconstriction. How do these changes help your body to maintain a constant internal temperature? *(6 marks)*

Exam tip

It is often helpful to structure long answers using bullet points – each bullet point should be worth one mark. In question 6c, there are six marks available, therefore your answer should contain six bullet points. Remember to ensure that each bullet point is a full written sentence.

C.1

Metals and non-metals

All substances are made out of **atoms**. These are tiny – around 1 000 000 atoms would fit across the width of a human hair. Atoms combine in a large variety of ways to produce all the substances on the Earth.

⇒ **1** *What are all substances made from?*

Elements

Some substances are only made out of one type of atom. These are called **elements**. There are just over 100 elements. Examples include copper and oxygen. All of the elements are listed on the **periodic table**.

⇒ **2** *What is an element?*

Metals and non-metals

Elements can be divided into **metals** and **non-metals**. Many metals share similar properties:

- they are strong
- they can be bent or hammered into different shapes
- they are good conductors of heat and electricity.

Around two-thirds of the elements in the periodic table are metals. Only the elements on the far right of the table are non-metals.

The 'staircase' (drawn in bold on the periodic table below) shows the divide between the metals and the non-metals. The elements to the left of this line are metals. The elements to the right of this line are non-metals.

Metals are found to the left of the 'staircase', non-metals to the right

⇒ **3** *How do you locate the position of non-metals on a periodic table?*

Key words: atom, element, periodic table, metal, non-metal

C.2

Structure of the atom

Atoms were once thought to be the smallest part of a substance that can exist. Although atoms are extremely small, they are made up of even smaller particles – the **subatomic particles**. There are three different types of subatomic particle.

1 *What is meant by a subatomic particle?*

Atoms consist of a central nucleus (**atomic nucleus**), with **electrons** orbiting it. The electrons are organised into energy levels, known as **electron shells**. (See C.12 Electron shells for more details.) An electron is an example of a subatomic particle.

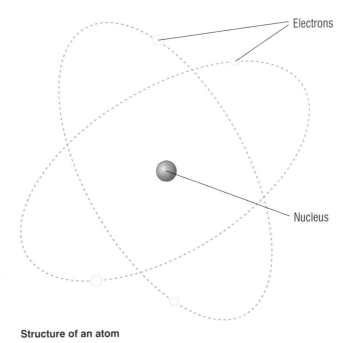

Electrons

Nucleus

Structure of an atom

2 *What is the name of the subatomic particle found orbiting the nucleus?*

3 *Where in an atom is the nucleus located?*

Key words: subatomic particle, atomic nucleus, electron, electron shell

C.3

Nucleus of an atom

The atomic nucleus is very small compared to the overall size of the atom.

(The diameter of a nucleus is only around $\frac{1}{10\,000}$th of the diameter of an atom. If an atom was as big as a cricket pitch, the nucleus would be about the size of a pea in the centre.)

The nucleus is found in the centre of the atom. It contains two types of subatomic particle – **protons** and **neutrons**. (Remember – electrons are the other type of subatomic particle.)

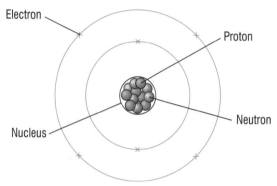

Protons and neutrons are found within an atom's tiny, central nucleus

→ 1 *Which two subatomic particles are found within the nucleus?*

Atomic symbols

The name of an element can vary, depending on the language you speak. Scientists all over the world study elements. It is important that all elements are represented using a code that is understood by all. Therefore each element is given a symbol – a one-letter, two-letter or less commonly, a three-letter code. (This is also easier to use as it is much shorter than an element's name!) These symbols are listed on the periodic table. For example:

- O = oxygen
- C = carbon
- Pb = lead (this comes from its Latin name – plumbum).

These symbols are also used to represent atoms in chemical formulae. For example, CO_2 is the chemical formula for carbon dioxide, and it shows that this molecule contains one carbon atom and two oxygen atoms.

→ 2 *Use the Periodic Table on the inside back cover of this book to find out the atomic symbol for hydrogen, nitrogen and sodium.*

Key words: proton, neutron

C.4

Atoms of elements

All the atoms of a particular element have the same number of protons. For example, carbon (C) has six protons in its nucleus. This means that every atom has six protons in its nucleus. By comparison, a hydrogen (H) atom has only one proton in its nucleus. The number of protons is unique to that element – no two elements have the same number of protons in their nucleus.

1 *What is special about the number of protons in an element?*

Atomic number

The number of protons in each atom of an element is known as its **atomic number**. The elements in the periodic table are arranged in order of their atomic number. This means they are arranged according to the number of protons they contain.

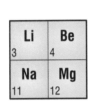

Elements are listed on a periodic table in order of their atomic number

To find out how many protons an element contains, refer to the periodic table. Once you have located your element, the atomic number (always the smaller of the two numbers, except for hydrogen where the values are the same) will tell you the number of protons in the nucleus. For example, sodium has 11 protons:

$$^{23}_{11}\text{Na}$$

Atomic number = 11

2 *How can you use the periodic table to work out the number of protons in an atom?*

Key word: atomic number

Exam tip

You do not need to remember how many protons there are in an atom of each of the elements. You just need to remember how to use the periodic table to work out how many protons an element contains. The atomic number is always the smaller of the two numbers printed next to an atom's symbol, except for hydrogen where the values are the same.

C.5

Atomic definitions

There are several key atomic definitions that you need to learn:

- **atomic number** – this is the number of protons present in the nucleus of an atom of an element
- **mass number** – this is the number of protons plus the number of neutrons present in the nucleus of an atom of an element
- **relative atomic mass** – this is a measure of the mass of one atom of an element. It is normally the same or very similar to the mass number of the element.

Relative masses are used – the mass of a single atom is so tiny that it would not be practical to use. Relative atomic masses are a measure of how heavy different atoms are compared to $\frac{1}{12}$th the mass of an atom of carbon-12. (For more details on relative atomic mass, see C.11 Calculating the relative atomic mass of isotopes.)

▶ **1** *What is the difference between atomic number and mass number?*

Key words: atomic number, mass number, relative atomic mass

C.6

Subatomic particles

Atoms are made up of subatomic particles; protons, neutrons and electrons (see C.2 Structure of the atom). Subatomic particles have different electrical charges and relative masses. These are summarised in the table below:

Particle	Relative charge	Relative mass
Proton	+1 (positive)	1
Neutron	0 (neutral – no charge)	1
Electron	−1 (negative)	Almost zero

As a nucleus contains protons and neutrons it has an overall positive charge.

▶ **1** *What is the relative mass of a proton?*

▶ **2** *What is the relative electrical charge on an electron?*

Key words: proton, neutron, electron

> **Bump up your grade**
>
> To remember the different charges subatomic particles have, use the start of the word to help you remember:
> - **p**rotons are **p**ositive
> - **neutr**ons are **neutr**al
> - electrons are left over, so they must be negative.

C.7

Numbers of subatomic particles

Atoms contain equal numbers of protons and electrons. For example, a nitrogen atom has seven protons, therefore it contains seven electrons. The positive charges of the protons cancel out the negative charges of the electrons. This means that an atom is neutral – it has no overall charge.

Remember, you can calculate how many protons an atom contains by looking up its **atomic number** on the periodic table. For example, how many protons and electrons are present in an atom of lithium?

Mass number =

Atomic number =

$$^{7}_{3}\text{Li}$$

How many protons are there? The atomic number of lithium is 3. This means that lithium contains 3 protons.

How many electrons are there? Atoms contain the same number of protons and electrons. This means that lithium contains 3 electrons.

Maths skills – How many neutrons?

The **mass number** of an element tells you the number of protons **plus** the number of neutrons present in an atom. We can use this to work out the number of neutrons using the formula below:

number of neutrons = mass number – atomic number

So, to calculate how many neutrons are present in a lithium atom:

number of neutrons = mass number – atomic number
= 7 – 3
= **4**

1 *If an atom contains 5 electrons, how many protons would it contain?*

2 *If an atom has 9 electrons and a mass number of 19, how many neutrons does it contain?*

Key words: atomic number, mass number

1 Draw a simple labelled diagram to show the structure of an atom.

2 Name three properties of a metal.

3 Match the chemical symbol to its name:
   a carbon   C
   b hydrogen   O
   c oxygen   H

4 Complete the table showing the relative charge and mass of subatomic particles.

Particle	Relative charge	Relative mass
Proton		
Neutron		
Electron		

5 How can you tell, from its position in the periodic table, if an element is a metal?

6 What is the difference between 'atomic number' and 'mass number'?

7 An atom of potassium has 19 protons. How many electrons does it contain?

8 Zinc has the following information in the periodic table: $^{65}_{30}$Zn.
   a What is the chemical symbol for zinc?
   b What is the mass number of zinc?
   c How many electrons are found in a zinc atom?

9 Use the following information taken from the periodic table about phosphorus, $^{31}_{15}$P, to answer these questions:
   a How many protons are found in an atom of phosphorus?
   b How many neutrons are found in an atom of phosphorus?
   c What is the overall charge of a phosphorus atom? Explain your answer.

C.8

The periodic table

Periods

Elements are arranged on the periodic table in order of their atomic number. They are arranged in order of increasing atomic number, going from left to right (you read across the table like reading a book). The rows of the periodic table are called **periods**. There are seven periods.

▮▶ **1** *What name is given to the rows going across the periodic table?*

Groups

The periodic table also has vertical columns called **groups**. There are eight groups (Groups 1–7 and Group 0). Elements within the same group have similar properties and react in similar ways. For example, Group 1 contains very reactive metals and Group 0 contains very unreactive gases called noble gases.

▮▶ **2** *What is the name of the vertical columns on the periodic table?*

Relative atomic mass | 1 | H | Atomic (proton) number | 1

Period numbers

Group numbers																0	Period numbers
1	2										3	4	5	6	7	4 He 2	1
7 Li 3	9 Be 4										11 B 5	12 C 6	14 N 7	16 O 8	19 F 9	20 Ne 10	2
23 Na 11	24 Mg 12										27 Al 13	28 Si 14	31 P 15	32 S 16	35.5 Cl 17	40 Ar 18	3
39 K 19	40 Ca 20	45 Sc 21	48 Ti 22	51 V 23	52 Cr 24	55 Mn 25	56 Fe 26	59 Co 27	59 Ni 28	63.5 Cu 29	65 Zn 30	70 Ga 31	73 Ge 32	75 As 33	79 Se 34	80 Br 35	84 Kr 36	4
85 Rb 37	88 Sr 38	89 Y 39	91 Zr 40	93 Nb 41	96 Mo 42	98 Tc 43	101 Ru 44	103 Rh 45	106 Pd 46	108 Ag 47	112 Cd 48	115 In 49	119 Sn 50	122 Sb 51	128 Te 52	127 I 53	131 Xe 54	5
133 Cs 55	137 Ba 56	139 La 57	178 Hf 72	181 Ta 73	184 W 74	186 Re 75	190 Os 76	192 Ir 77	195 Pt 78	197 Au 79	201 Hg 80	204 Tl 81	207 Pb 82	209 Bi 83	209 Po 84	210 At 85	222 Rn 86	6
223 Fr 87	226 Ra 88	227 Ac 89																

Elements 58–71 and 90–103 (all metals) have been omitted

Key

■ **Reactive metals** These metals react vigorously with other elements.

■ **Non-metals** These elements have low melting and boiling points, and many are liquids or gases at room temperature and pressure.

☐ **Transition elements** These metals are not usually very reactive – some, like silver and gold, are very unreactive.

■ **Noble gases** These (non-metal) elements are very unreactive, and it is very difficult to get them to combine with other elements.

■ **Other metals**

The modern periodic table

▮▶ **3** *Which period and group is argon (Ar) found in?*

Key words: period, group

C.9

Isotopes

Atoms of the same element always contain the same number of **protons** (and therefore electrons) and you will recall that this is the same as the atomic number of the element (see C.4 Atoms of elements). However, different versions of an atom exist and they have different numbers of **neutrons.** These are called **isotopes.**

> **1** *What is an isotope?*

Chemical properties of isotopes

The isotopes of an element have the same chemical properties – they will react in the same way. This is because as well as having the same number of protons, they will also have the same number of electrons. They only differ in the number of neutrons. The way in which an atom reacts depends on its electronic structure (see C.13 Groups on the periodic table). As the isotopes of an element have the same number of electrons, they will have the same electronic structure, and because of this, they react in the same way.

> **2** *Why do isotopes react in the same way?*

Physical properties of isotopes

The physical properties of isotopes are different. For example, they have different densities. Some isotopes are radioactive. This occurs if the extra neutrons in its nucleus make it unstable.

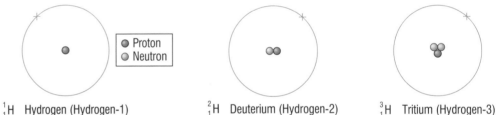

$^{1}_{1}$H Hydrogen (Hydrogen-1) $^{2}_{1}$H Deuterium (Hydrogen-2) $^{3}_{1}$H Tritium (Hydrogen-3)

Hydrogen has three isotopes – hydrogen, deuterium and tritium. They have identical chemical properties. They can all react with oxygen to produce water. However, they have different physical properties. For example, tritium is radioactive.

C.10

Relative atomic mass of isotopes

Atomic number of isotopes

Isotopes always have the same **atomic number**. This is because the atomic number is the same as the number of protons in the nucleus of an atom. (Remember – atoms of the same element always contain the same number of protons.) For example, all isotopes of hydrogen have an atomic number of 1.

Mass number of isotopes

Isotopes have different **mass numbers**. This is because the mass number is the total of the protons and neutrons present in the nucleus of an atom. All isotopes of a particular element will have a different number of neutrons, and therefore will have a different mass number. For example, deuterium (hydrogen-2) has a mass number of 2, whereas the mass number of tritium (hydrogen-3) is 3.

Key words: isotopes, atomic number, mass number, relative atomic mass

▷ **1** *Why do isotopes have different mass numbers?*

Relative atomic mass of isotopes

The **relative atomic mass** of an element takes into account any common isotopes of an element that are found naturally. It is calculated by finding out the average mass of all the different isotopes, according to the proportion of each isotope that is present in a natural mixture of the element (see C.11 Calculating the relative atomic mass of isotopes). This means that the relative atomic mass of an element is not always a whole number. (However, it is often rounded to the nearest whole number when displayed on a periodic table.)

C.11

Key points

- Relative atomic mass has the symbol A_r.
- The relative atomic mass of an element can be found as the mass number from the periodic table.
- To calculate the A_r of an element, work out the percentage of each isotope present and add them together.

Element	A_r
H – hydrogen	1
C – carbon	12
O – oxygen	16
Mg – magnesium	24

▷ **1** *Name an element with a greater relative atomic mass than carbon.*

▷ **2** *Name an element with a smaller relative atomic mass than carbon.*

Key word: relative atomic mass

Calculating the relative atomic mass of isotopes

Relative atomic mass

Different atoms have different masses. As their mass is so small, scientists study the size of one atom relative to another. The **relative atomic mass** of an atom tells us how heavy an atom is compared with $\frac{1}{12}$th the mass of an atom of carbon-12.

(Carbon-12 is one isotope of carbon.)

Relative atomic mass is often shortened to the symbol A_r. The A_r of carbon is 12. Atoms with an A_r less than 12 have a smaller mass than a carbon atom. Atoms with an A_r larger than 12 have a mass greater than a carbon atom.

From the table in the margin you can tell that magnesium atoms have twice the mass of carbon atoms. The A_r values also allow you to work out that sixteen hydrogen atoms have the same mass as one oxygen atom.

Maths skills – Calculating relative atomic mass

The relative atomic mass of an element containing two isotopes can be calculated using the following formula:

$$\begin{array}{c}\text{relative atomic} \\ \text{mass}\end{array} = \left(\begin{array}{c}\text{proportion} \\ \text{of isotope 1}\end{array} \times \begin{array}{c}A_r \text{ of} \\ \text{isotope 1}\end{array}\right) + \left(\begin{array}{c}\text{proportion} \\ \text{of isotope 2}\end{array} \times \begin{array}{c}A_r \text{ of} \\ \text{isotope 2}\end{array}\right)$$

The proportion of an isotope is the percentage abundance, expressed as a decimal, e.g. 60% = 0.6.

Worked example

Chlorine has two naturally occurring isotopes: chlorine-35 ($^{35}_{17}$Cl) and chlorine-37 ($^{37}_{17}$Cl). In a naturally occurring sample of chlorine gas, 75% of the mixture is chlorine-35, and 25% of the mixture is chlorine-37. Calculate the relative atomic mass of chlorine.

$$\begin{array}{c}\text{relative atomic} \\ \text{mass}\end{array} = \left(\begin{array}{c}\text{proportion} \\ \text{of isotope 1}\end{array} \times \begin{array}{c}A_r \text{ of} \\ \text{isotope 1}\end{array}\right) + \left(\begin{array}{c}\text{proportion} \\ \text{of isotope 2}\end{array} \times \begin{array}{c}A_r \text{ of} \\ \text{isotope 2}\end{array}\right)$$

$$= \quad (0.75 \times 35) \quad + \quad (0.25 \times 37)$$

$$= \textbf{35.5}$$

So, the relative atomic mass of chlorine is 35.5.

C.12

Key points

- The electrons in an atom are arranged in energy levels, known as electron shells.
- The lowest energy level – the shell nearest to the nucleus – is always filled first.
- Only a certain number of electrons are allowed in a shell – 2 in the first, 8 in the second, and 8 in the third.

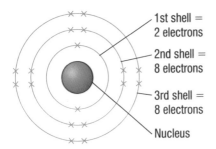

1st shell = 2 electrons

2nd shell = 8 electrons

3rd shell = 8 electrons

Nucleus

An electron shell diagram

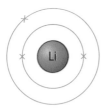

A lithium atom

Electron shells

The electrons in an atom are arranged in different levels, known as **electron shells**. Each electron shell represents a different energy level. The electron shell nearest to the nucleus is the lowest energy level. Electrons in an atom always fill the lowest energy level first (the electron shell closest to the nucleus).

 1 *Where would you find the electron shell containing the lowest energy level?*

Electron shell diagrams

An electron shell diagram is often used to show the position of electrons in an atom. This is also known as an atom's **electronic configuration**. An energy shell can only contain a certain number of electrons:

- first shell (lowest energy level) – can hold up to 2 electrons
- second shell – can hold up to 8 electrons
- third shell – can hold up to 8 electrons.

After this, any extra electrons go into the fourth shell. You only need to be able to draw the electron shell diagrams for the first twenty elements.

2 *How many electrons can the second electron shell hold?*

Filling electron shells

Electrons always fill the electron shells from the lowest energy level, outwards. So if an element has only got one electron, it will be found in the first electron shell. However, if an element has five electrons, two electrons will be found in the first energy level, and the remaining three electrons in the second electron shell.

The third element in the periodic table is lithium. It has an atomic number of 3. From this information we know that it has three protons. This also means that it has three electrons; two electrons in the first electron shell and one electron in the second electron shell.

Electronic configuration

The electronic configuration of an atom can also be represented by listing the number of electrons in each energy level. This always starts with the lowest energy level (the electron shell closest to the nucleus), working outwards. Lithium, for example, has an electronic configuration of 2.1.

3 *What is an atom's electronic configuration?*

Electron shells and electronic configurations

Element	Symbol	Number of electrons	Electron shell diagram	Electronic configuration
Hydrogen	^1_1H	1		1
Boron	$^{11}_5B$	5		2.3
Oxygen	$^{16}_8O$	8		2.6
Sodium	$^{23}_{11}Na$	11		2.8.1
Argon	$^{40}_{18}Ar$	18		2.8.8
Calcium	$^{40}_{20}Ca$	20		2.8.8.2

Key words: electron shells, electronic configuration

C.13

Groups on the periodic table

Groups

Elements in the periodic table are arranged into **groups**. There are eight groups: Groups 1–7 and Group 0 (see C.8 The periodic table).

Elements within the same group of the periodic table react in similar ways. This is because their atoms have the same number of electrons in their outermost shell (the highest energy level).

Atoms of elements gain, lose or share electrons when they react with other atoms. The group number tells us how many electrons are present in the outermost shell of the atom:

Elements in Group 1 have only one electron in their outermost electron shell. These elements can lose this electron easily – this makes these elements very reactive.

Group 1

All elements in Group 1 have one electron in their outermost shell

Group	Number of electrons in outermost shell
1	1
2	2
3	3
4	4
5	5
6	6
7	7
0	Full

Elements in Group 0 have a full outermost electron shell. These elements do not lose or gain electrons – this makes them very unreactive.

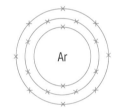

Argon has a full outermost shell of electrons, in this case 8, as the third shell can hold 8 electrons

1 *How many electrons are found in the outermost shell of an element belonging to Group 3?*

2 *How many electrons are found in the outermost shell of an element belonging to Group 6?*

Periods

Elements are also arranged into rows in the periodic table, known as **periods** (see C.8). The period number tells you the number of **electron shells**, containing electrons, which surround the nucleus of an atom. For example, elements in period 2 have two electron shells which contain electrons.

3 *How many electron shells, containing electrons, would an atom of an element found in period 3 contain?*

1 Two elements have similar chemical properties. Will they be found in the same group or the same period in the periodic table?

2 How many electrons would be found in the outermost shell of an element found in Group 7?

3 Choose the most appropriate words to complete the following sentence: Electrons in the first electron shell (lowest energy level) are found *closest to/ furthest from* the nucleus.

4 Draw electron shell diagrams for:

   a carbon (it has 6 electrons)

   b magnesium (12th in the periodic table)

   c silicon (atomic number 14)

   d phosphorus (Group 5, period 3).

5 Write down the electronic configuration for each example in question 4 above.

6 Give an example of how two isotopes of an element may be different from each other.

7 Explain why isotopes have the same chemical properties, but different physical properties.

8 Explain why some elements have a relative atomic mass that is not a whole number (for example, A_r for copper = 63.5).

9 In a naturally occurring mixture of lithium, 8% is lithium-6 and 92% is lithium-7. Calculate the relative atomic mass of lithium.

Checklist	✓ ✓ ✓
Tick when you have:	
reviewed it after your lesson ☑ ☐ ☐	The periodic table ☐ ☐ ☐
revised once – some questions right ☑ ☑ ☐	Isotopes ☐ ☐ ☐
revised twice – all questions right ☑ ☑ ☑	Relative atomic mass of isotopes ☐ ☐ ☐
Move on to another topic when you have all three ticks	Calculating the relative atomic mass of isotopes ☐ ☐ ☐
	Electron shells ☐ ☐ ☐
	Groups on the periodic table ☐ ☐ ☐

1 The diagram shows the structure of a boron atom:

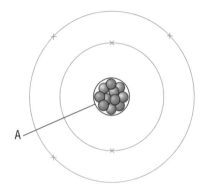

a i What is structure A on the diagram? *(1 mark)*

   ii Name the **two** types of subatomic particle found in structure A. *(2 marks)*

b i How many electrons are present in a boron atom? *(1 mark)*

   ii What is the relative charge on an electron? *(1 mark)*

Use the periodic table to:

c i Name another element in the same group as boron. *(1 mark)*

   ii State and explain if boron is a metal or a non-metal. *(2 marks)*

Exam tip

You do not need to learn all the information on the periodic table, just how to use it. If a question requires you to refer to the periodic table, this will be provided in your exam.

2 a Choose appropriate words to complete the following sentences on atoms.

All elements consist of .... type of atom.

Atoms consist of a nucleus found in the .... of an atom.

Electrons surround the nucleus in ....

Electrons in the lowest energy level are found .... to the nucleus. *(4 marks)*

b Complete the following table about the subatomic particles found in an atom.
Some of the answers have been filled in for you.

Particle	Relative charge	Relative mass
Proton		1
Neutron		1
Electron	−1	

(3 marks)

3 Use the following information taken from the periodic table about iron:

$$^{56}_{26}\text{Fe}$$

a What is the chemical symbol for iron? *(1 mark)*

b i What is the atomic number of iron? *(1 mark)*

   ii How many protons are found in an atom of iron? *(1 mark)*

   iii How many neutrons are found in an atom of iron? Show your working. *(2 marks)*

c What is the overall charge on an iron atom? Explain your answer. *(2 marks)*

Exam tip

Remember, the atomic number is always the smaller of the two numbers printed next to an atom's symbol in the periodic table. The mass number is always the largest.

4 Use the following information taken from the periodic table about nitrogen:

$$^{14}_{7}N$$

a What is the mass number of nitrogen? *(1 mark)*

b **i** How many electrons does an atom of nitrogen contain? *(1 mark)*

ii Complete the diagram below to show the electron configuration of a nitrogen atom. Use an 'x' to represent an electron. *(2 marks)*

c **i** Phosphorus is found in the same group as nitrogen. What does this tell you about phosphorus? *(1 mark)*

ii To which group do both phosphorus and nitrogen belong? *(1 mark)*

iii What does the group number tell you about the electron arrangement of an atom? *(1 mark)*

d Phosphorus has an atomic number of 15. What is its electronic configuration? *(2 marks)*

5 There are two naturally occurring forms of copper:

$$^{63}_{29}Cu \qquad ^{65}_{29}Cu$$

a **i** State **one** way in which the atomic structure of these atoms is the same. *(1 mark)*

ii State **one** way in which the atomic structure of these atoms differs. *(1 mark)*

b **i** What are these two atoms of copper known as? *(1 mark)*

ii State and explain **one** similarity and **one** difference between the properties of these two atoms. *(4 marks)*

c Why is the relative atomic mass of copper not a whole number? *(2 marks)*

6 The table below shows the naturally occurring isotopes of magnesium:

Isotope	Mass number	Relative abundance
Magnesium-24	24	79%
Magnesum-25	25	10%
Magnesium-26	26	11%

a **i** What is the chemical symbol for magnesium? *(1 mark)*

ii Magnesium has an atomic number of 12. How many neutrons does magnesium-26 contain? *(1 mark)*

iii What is the electron configuration of magnesium? *(2 marks)*

b Calculate the relative atomic mass of magnesium. *(3 marks)*

D.1

Key points

- The periodic table lists all the elements. It can be used to tell you both an element's name and symbol.
- Chemical formulae tell us the types and number of the atoms present in a molecule.

Key words: chemical symbol, molecule, chemical formula, compound

Bump up your grade

It is helpful to learn the symbols of common elements. This will save you time in exams as you won't have to look them up on the periodic table.

⟫ **1** *What is the chemical symbol for potassium?*

⟫ **2** *What is the name of the element that is represented by the symbol Al?*

A molecule of carbon dioxide (CO_2) has one carbon atom (black) and two oxygen atoms (red)

⟫ **3** *The gas methane has the chemical formula CH_4. Which atoms is this molecule made up of?*

Using the periodic table to recognise elements and formulae of simple compounds

Chemical symbols

Each atom has its own **chemical symbol**. For example, O stands for oxygen and He stands for helium. The first letter of a symbol is always a capital letter. If a symbol has a second letter, it is always a lowercase letter.

You can use the periodic table to find out the name of an element if you are given its symbol. Alternatively, if you are given the symbol, you can find out an element's name.

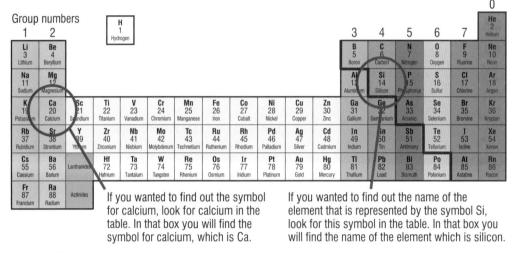

If you wanted to find out the symbol for calcium, look for calcium in the table. In that box you will find the symbol for calcium, which is Ca.

If you wanted to find out the name of the element that is represented by the symbol Si, look for this symbol in the table. In that box you will find the name of the element which is silicon.

The periodic table

Chemical formulae

Not all atoms exist on their own. They may be joined to other atoms to form **molecules**. The **chemical formula** (plural – formulae) of a molecule tells you which atoms are in the molecule. (Remember, if you don't know which element a symbol represents, look it up on the periodic table.) For example, the chemical formula for common salt (sodium chloride) is NaCl. Molecules that are made up of more than one element are known as **compounds** (see D.2 Elements, compounds, mixtures and molecules and D.14 Common chemical formulae).

$$\text{Na represents sodium} \longrightarrow \text{NaCl} \longleftarrow \text{Cl represents chlorine}$$

This formula tells us that salt (sodium chloride) is a compound, containing one sodium atom and one chlorine atom.

The chemical formula also tells you how many of each atom there are in a molecule. For example, the chemical formula for water is H_2O. This tells you that there are two hydrogen (H) atoms in a molecule of water. The number is always given as a subscript, in other words written below the line of text.

If no number is written, this means that there is only one of this type of atom in the molecule. For example, the chemical formula for carbon dioxide is CO_2:

$$\text{There is one atom of carbon} \longrightarrow \text{CO}_2 \longleftarrow \text{There are two atoms of oxygen}$$

This formula tells us that carbon dioxide is a molecule, containing one carbon atom and two oxygen atoms.

D.2

Key points

- Elements contain only one type of atom.
- Compounds contain more than one type of atom bonded together.
- Molecules consist of more than one atom bonded together. Molecules can be either elements or compounds.
- Mixtures are made up of more than one type of element or compound, which are not bonded together.

Key words: element, compound, molecule, mixture

Elements, compounds, mixtures and molecules

Elements

Elements are made up of only one type of atom. There are just over 100 different elements.

Compounds

Compounds contain more than one type of atom. The different atoms are chemically bonded together. This makes it very difficult to separate a compound back into its elements. The properties of a compound are completely different to the properties of the elements it was made from.

▐▶ **1** *What is a compound?*

Molecules

Molecules consist of more than one atom chemically bonded together. There are two main groups of molecules:

- molecules of elements – these molecules contain more than one atom of the same element bonded together. These are also known as molecular elements.
- molecules of compounds – these molecule contain more than one type of atom bonded together. They are made up of more than one element.

▐▶ **2** *What are molecules?*

Mixtures

Most materials are **mixtures**. Mixtures have two things in common:

- they contain more than one type of substance – these can be elements, compounds or both
- the different substances are not bonded together.

Mixtures are easier to separate than compounds, as the substances they contain are not bonded together.

▐▶ **3** *What is a mixture?*

Carbon is an element – it only contains carbon atoms

Carbon dioxide is a compound – it is made up of carbon and oxygen atoms chemically bonded together

Oxygen molecules (O_2) are an example of molecules of an element

Water molecules (H_2O) are an example of molecules of a compound

Air is an example of a mixture – it contains carbon dioxide, nitrogen and oxygen molecules, as well as a small number of other gases

D.3

Key points

- Reactants are the chemicals that combine together during a chemical reaction.
- Products are the new substances made by a chemical reaction.
- Word equations show how reactants combine together to form the products in a chemical reaction.

Word equations

Reactants and products

When two substances join together to make a compound, a chemical reaction takes place. We can show what happens during a chemical reaction using a **word equation**:

- the substances which take part in the chemical reaction are known as the **reactants**
- the new substances produced as a result of the chemical reaction are called the **products**.

▶ **1** *What is meant by a reactant?*

▶ **2** *What is meant by a product?*

Writing a word equation

Word equations for chemical reactions are always written in the same way:

reactants ——————————————→ products
(the arrow represents the chemical reaction taking place)

For example, hydrogen will react with oxygen to form water. The compound formed is chemically known as hydrogen oxide, but we normally refer to it as water.

hydrogen + oxygen ——————→ water
(reactants) (product)

Naming compounds

One way to make a compound is to react a metal element with a non-metal element. The compound is named in two parts:

- first part of the compound name – the metal name from the reactants
- second part of the compound name – the ending of the non-metal is changed to -**ide**.

For example,

copper + oxygen ——————→ copper ox**ide**
iron + sulfur ——————→ iron sulf**ide**

▶ **3** *What compound is formed if you react sodium and chlorine?*

Some compound names end in -**ate** meaning that oxygen is in the compound.

For example,

sodium + carbon + oxygen ——————→ sodium carbon**ate**

Key words: word equation, reactant, product

D.4

Balanced chemical equations

Key points

- Balanced chemical equations show how much of a substance is reacting.
- During a chemical reaction, atoms are not made or destroyed.
- The total mass of the products formed is the same as the total mass of the reactants.

Balanced chemical equations (symbol equations) show you how much of each substance is reacting in a chemical reaction. It is better to represent a chemical reaction as a balanced chemical equation, rather than a word equation, because:
- it tells us how much of each substance is involved in the reaction
- everyone can understand the reaction regardless of the language they speak
- it is much shorter to write.

For example,

magnesium + chlorine ⟶ magnesium chloride (word equation)

$Mg + Cl_2 \longrightarrow MgCl_2$ (balanced chemical equation)

▶ **1** *What does a chemical equation reaction tell us?*

Bump up your grade

Note – it is not possible to alter the numbers within the formula of a compound, as this changes the type of compound you have.

Bump up your grade

Practise balancing chemical equations, as you may be asked to do this in an exam. Work through the equation slowly, back and forth between products and reactants, until you have equal numbers of each type of atom on both sides of the equation.

Balanced equations

During a chemical reaction, atoms are not created or destroyed. This means that the mass of the products formed from a chemical reaction is the same as the mass of the reactants.

Total mass of reactants = total mass of products

An equation is said to be **balanced** when there is the same number of each type of atom on both sides of the equation.

An example of a balanced chemical equation is when calcium carbonate (limestone) is heated and decomposes (breaks down) into calcium oxide and carbon dioxide:

Key words: chemical equation, balanced equation

calcium carbonate ⟶ calcium oxide + carbon dioxide

$CaCO_3 \longrightarrow CaO + CO_2$

Reactants: 1 atom of Ca   Products: 1 atom of Ca
1 atom of C   1 atom of C
3 atoms of O   3 atoms of O

▶ **2** *What is meant by a balanced chemical equation?*

Maths skills – Balancing an equation

Balance the equation for making hydrochloric acid (HCl):

hydrogen + chlorine → hydrochloric acid

Step 1 – Write out the formula of each reactant and each product:

$H_2 + Cl_2 \rightarrow HCl$

Step 2 – Count how many atoms are present on each side of the equation:

Reactants: Products:
2 atoms of hydrogen   1 atom of hydrogen
2 atoms of chlorine   1 atom of chlorine

If at this stage there are equal numbers of each type of atom on both sides of the equation, the equation is balanced. In this case, the equation is not balanced.

Step 3 – Balance the equation by adding numbers in front of the formulae of the different compounds. This changes the number of molecules of each compound you have.

In this example we need another atom of hydrogen and another atom of chlorine on the products side of the equation. To do this we put a **2** in front of the hydrochloric acid molecule. This means that there are now 2 hydrochloric acid molecules produced by the reaction.

$H_2 + Cl_2 \rightarrow 2HCl$

Step 4 – Check that the equation now balances, by counting how many atoms are present on each side of the equation:

Reactants: Products:
2 atoms of hydrogen   2 atom of hydrogen
2 atoms of oxygen   2 atom of oxygen

There is the same number of each type of atom on both sides of the equation, therefore the equation is balanced.

The balanced chemical equation now tells us that 1 molecule of hydrogen will react with 1 molecule of chlorine to form 2 molecules of hydrochloric acid.

Key points

- When chemicals react, new products are made.
- Products made through chemical reactions include acids, alkalis and salts.
- Salts are metal compounds formed from an acid.

Salt – sodium chloride

Reactions with acids, alkalis and salts

When chemicals react, many useful **products** are made. These include **acids**, **bases** and **salts**.

 1 *What is the general name given to a substance made as a result of a chemical reaction?*

Salts

The name salt is given to any metal compound that can be made from an acid. This means that it contains metal atoms bonded to atoms of at least one other element. The most common example of a salt is table salt (often put on chips!). Table salt's chemical name is sodium chloride. This tells us that it is made from sodium atoms and chlorine atoms.

 2 *What does the term 'salt' mean?*

The table below shows a range of useful products that can be made from chemical reactions:

Acid	Alkali	Salt
Hydrochloric acid – found in your stomach	Sodium hydroxide – found in oven cleaner	Ammonium nitrate – used as a fertiliser
Ethanoic acid – vinegar	Slaked lime – added to neutralise acidic soil	Iron sulfate – used on lawns to kill moss
Citric acid – found in lemons	Ammonia – found in kitchen cleaners	Calcium sulfate – used to make plaster
Sulfuric acid – found in car batteries	Antacid tablets – used to treat indigestion	Sodium chloride – used as a flavour enhancer in foods
A range of products containing acids	A range of products containing alkalis	Ammonium nitrate is an example of a salt used as a fertiliser

Key words: products, acids, bases, salts

Acids, bases and alkalis

Acids, bases and alkalis are found in the laboratory and at home. They vary in strength. For example, some acids can be eaten, whereas others can be irritants or corrosive and must be handled carefully.

Acid and alkali strength is measured using the **pH scale**. The scale ranges from pH 0 – most acidic, to pH 14 – most alkaline. Solutions with a pH of 7 are neutral. (See D.11 pH tests using universal indicator and litmus, for more information on pH.)

Chemicals can be identified as acids or bases using indicators such as litmus and universal indicator. (See D.11 pH tests using universal indicator and litmus.)

Acids

Acids have a number of key features:
- they taste sour – though many are too harmful to taste
- they have a pH less than 7
- when they are dissolved in water they form hydrogen ions (positively charged hydrogen atoms, H^+).

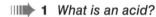 **1** *What is an acid?*

Bases

Bases are substances that react with acids and neutralise them. They have a pH of more than 7. Many bases are insoluble (they do not dissolve) in water. Some bases can dissolve in water – these are called **alkalis**.

For example, copper oxide is a base as it can be used to neutralise acids. However, it is not an alkali because it does not dissolve in water.

Sodium hydroxide is a base as it can be used to neutralise acids. It is also an alkali because it's soluble (dissolves) in water.

2 *What is a base?*

Alkalis

Alkalis have a number of key features:
- they feel soapy – though many are irritants so should not come into contact with your skin
- they have a pH more than 7
- when they are dissolved in water they form hydroxide ions (negatively charged hydroxide molecules, OH^-).

3 *What is an alkali?*

Solutions

When an acid is dissolved in water, an acidic solution is formed.

When an alkali is dissolved in water, an alkaline solution is formed.

If a solution is neither acidic nor alkaline, a **neutral** solution is formed. Pure water and paraffin are examples of neutral solutions. Neutral solutions have a pH of 7.

1 Sort the following list into acids and alkalis:
sodium hydroxide, hydrochloric acid, ammonia, lemon juice.

2 In the following word equation:
zinc + oxygen → zinc oxide,

   a name the product

   b name the reactants.

3 What is the difference between an element and a compound?

4 What is the difference between a base and an alkali?

5 Why are mixtures easier to separate than compounds?

6 How many atoms of copper, sulfur and oxygen are found in one molecule of copper sulfate ($CuSO_4$)?

7 Which ions are formed when acids and alkalis dissolve in water?

8 Balance the following equation: $H_2 + O_2 \rightarrow H_2O$

9 Balance the following equation: $Al + O_2 \rightarrow Al_2O_3$

Checklist ✓ ✓ ✓

Tick when you have:

reviewed it after your lesson	✓	☐	☐
revised once – some questions right	✓	✓	☐
revised twice – all questions right	✓	✓	✓

Move on to another topic when you have all three ticks

Using the periodic table to recognise elements and formulae of simple compounds	☐	☐	☐
Elements, compounds, mixtures and molecules	☐	☐	☐
Word equations	☐	☐	☐
Balanced chemical equations	☐	☐	☐
Reactions with acids, alkalis and salts	☐	☐	☐
Acids, bases and alkalis	☐	☐	☐

D.7

Key points

- Acids and bases neutralise each other – forming a neutral solution of a salt and water.
- A neutralisation reaction can be represented by: acid + base → salt + water

Key words: neutralisation, salt

Neutralisation

Acids and bases are chemical opposites. They react together and 'cancel each other out'. If you mix together the right amount of acid and alkali, a neutral solution is produced. This type of reaction is known as a **neutralisation** reaction. The neutral solution produced will have a pH of 7. Universal indicator would show a green colour. (For more details see D.11 pH tests using universal indicator and litmus.)

The neutralisation reaction can be represented by the word equation:

acid + base → salt + water

▶ **1** *What happens during a neutralisation reaction?*

Making salts

When an acid reacts with a base, a **salt** and water are produced. The type of salt produced depends on the type of base and acid used. Many bases are metal oxides, for example, copper oxide and zinc oxide. These substances do not dissolve in water. However, bases that do dissolve in water (alkalis), such as sodium hydroxide, can also be used to neutralise an acid.

Naming salts

The name of a salt consists of two parts. The first part of the name comes from the metal in the metal oxide or hydroxide. The second part of the name comes from the acid that the base reacted with:

- salts made from hydrochloric acid end in chloride
- salts made from sulfuric acid end in sulfate
- salts made from nitric acid end in nitrate.

The neutralisation reaction is shown below for the reaction between hydrochloric acid + copper oxide:

▶ **2** *Which type of salt is made from a reaction involving nitric acid?*

acid + base → salt + water (general word equation)

hydrochloric acid + copper oxide → copper chloride + water (word equation)

$2HCl + CuO \rightarrow CuCl_2 + H_2O$ (balanced chemical equation)

The following table provides a summary of the name of the salt produced by different reactions between acids and metal bases.

Acid	Base	Salt produced + water
Sulfuric acid	Copper oxide	Copper sulfate + water
Nitric acid	Copper oxide	Copper nitrate + water
Hydrochloric acid	Zinc oxide	Zinc chloride + water
Sulfuric acid	Zinc oxide	Zinc sulfate + water
Nitric acid	Zinc oxide	Zinc nitrate + water
Hydrochloric acid	Sodium hydroxide	Sodium chloride + water
Sulfuric acid	Sodium hydroxide	Sodium sulfate + water
Nitric acid	Sodium hydroxide	Sodium nitrate + water

▶ **3** *Write the word equation for the reaction between sulfuric acid and zinc oxide.*

Bump up your grade

Remember alkalis are a subset of bases – they are bases that can dissolve in water. Neutralisation can also be represented by the word equation:

acid + alkali → salt + water

Exam tip

Learn all the equations on this page; you could be asked about any of these neutralisation reactions in your exam.

D.8

Key points

- When an acid reacts with a metal, a salt and hydrogen are produced.
- Acid + metal → salt + hydrogen

Key word: salt

Reacting acids and metals

Salts can be made by reacting metals with acids. However, this is only possible if the metal is more reactive than hydrogen. For example, copper is less reactive than hydrogen so will not react with an acid to form a salt.

If the metal is more reactive than hydrogen, then it will react to produce a salt and hydrogen gas. This reaction can be represented by the word equation:

acid + metal → salt + hydrogen

▏▎▍▶ **1** *What gas is always produced if you react a metal with an acid?*

For example, if you react hydrochloric acid with magnesium:

acid	+	metal	→	salt	+	hydrogen (general word equation)
hydrochloric acid	+	magnesium	→	magnesium chloride	+	hydrogen (word equation)
$2HCl$	+	Mg	→	$MgCl_2$	+	H_2	(balanced chemical equation)

Rates of reaction

The more reactive a metal is, the faster and more violent the reaction is with an acid. You can tell the speed of a reaction by the rate at which hydrogen bubbles are given off. In the photograph below, magnesium is the most reactive metal and copper the least. It is less reactive than hydrogen, so no reaction is occurring.

Sulfuric acid + iron → iron sulfate + hydrogen

Sulfuric acid + magnesium → magnesium sulfate + hydrogen

Copper is less reactive than hydrogen, so no reaction occurs when it is placed in sulfuric acid.

Reacting metals with acids

You would never react Group 1 metals, such as sodium and potassium, with an acid as the reaction is too violent to carry out safely.

▏▎▍▶ **2** *Why does copper not react with acid to form a salt?*

Bump up your grade

Remember if a metal reacts with hydrochloric acid, chloride salts are always produced. Whereas, if a metal reacts with sulfuric acid, sulfate salts are always produced.

D.9

Key points

- Acids can be neutralised by reacting them with carbonates.
- Acid + carbonate → salt + water + carbon dioxide

Reacting acids and carbonates

Acids can also be neutralised by reacting them with **carbonates**. Carbonates contain carbon and oxygen atoms in their compounds. All carbonates contain the carbonate (CO_3^{2-}) ion. For example, limestone is a type of carbonate – it is called calcium carbonate ($CaCO_3$).

The reaction between acids and carbonates can be summarised in the word equation:

$$acid + carbonate \rightarrow salt + water + carbon\ dioxide$$

➤ **1** *What gas is always produced when an acid reacts with a carbonate?*

For example, calcium carbonate (limestone) reacts with hydrochloric acid to form calcium chloride, water and carbon dioxide:

acid	+ carbonate →	salt	+ water +	carbon dioxide
hydrochloric acid	+ calcium carbonate →	calcium chloride	+ water +	carbon dioxide
$2HCl$	+ $CaCO_3$ →	$CaCl_2$	+ H_2O +	CO_2

➤ **2** *Which group of salts will always be produced if a carbonate reacts with hydrochloric acid?*

Remember the salt that is produced depends upon which acid and which metal carbonate react.

The following table provides a summary of the name of the salt produced by different reactions between acids and metal carbonates.

Acid	Carbonate	Salt produced + water + carbon dioxide
Sulfuric acid	Calcium carbonate	Calcium sulfate + water + carbon dioxide
Nitric acid	Calcium carbonate	Calcium nitrate + water + carbon dioxide
Hydrochloric acid	Copper carbonate	Copper chloride + water + carbon dioxide
Sulfuric acid	Copper carbonate	Copper sulfate + water + carbon dioxide
Nitric acid	Copper carbonate	Copper nitrate + water + carbon dioxide
Hydrochloric acid	Sodium carbonate	Sodium chloride + water + carbon dioxide
Sulfuric acid	Sodium carbonate	Sodium sulfate + water + carbon dioxide
Nitric acid	Sodium carbonate	Sodium nitrate + water + carbon dioxide

➤ **3** *Write the word equation for the reaction between sulfuric acid and copper carbonate.*

Exam tip

Learn all the equations on this page as you could be asked about any of these neutralisation reactions in your exam.

Key word: carbonate

Chemical tests for hydrogen and carbon dioxide

Testing for hydrogen

Hydrogen gas is less dense than air and has no colour or smell. It can be collected using a gas syringe or by placing a test tube upside down in water.

Zinc is reacting with hydrochloric acid to produce hydrogen and zinc chloride. The hydrogen gas is collecting at the top of the test tube.

Once collected, the gas can be tested by placing a lighted splint into the top of the test tube of water. If hydrogen is present a squeaky pop is produced when the gas burns. The 'squeaky pop' is the sound of a small explosion – hydrogen is highly **flammable**!

▐▐▌➡ **1** *How do you test for the presence of hydrogen?*

Testing for carbon dioxide

To test for carbon dioxide, gas is bubbled through lime water. If carbon dioxide is present the lime water turns cloudy.

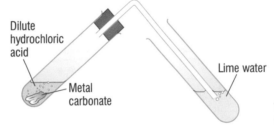

Dilute hydrochloric acid

Metal carbonate

Lime water

When acids react with metal carbonates, carbon dioxide is released. This turns lime water cloudy.

Lime water is a solution of calcium hydroxide. When it reacts with carbon dioxide, calcium carbonate is produced. This is insoluble and makes the solution appear cloudy.

lime water + carbon dioxide → calcium carbonate + water
(calcium hydroxide)

$$Ca(OH)_2 \quad + \quad CO_2(g) \quad \rightarrow \quad CaCO_3(s) \quad + \quad H_2O$$

▐▐▌➡ **2** *How do you test for the presence of carbon dioxide?*

D.11

- Indicators change colour to show whether a solution is acidic or alkaline.
- Litmus paper turns red in acidic solutions.
- Litmus paper turns blue in alkaline solutions.
- Universal indicator turns a range of colours, from red in acidic solutions through to blue in alkaline solutions. It can therefore be used to measure the pH of a solution.

Acids turn blue litmus paper red

Alkalis turn red litmus paper blue

Key words: indicator, litmus paper, universal indicator, pH scale

pH tests using universal indicator and litmus

Indicators can be used to determine if a solution is acidic (pH less than 7) or alkaline (pH greater than 7). The colour of an indicator will show whether the solution is acidic or alkaline. **Litmus paper** and **universal indicator** are two examples of indicators.

▶ **1** *What is an indicator?*

Litmus paper

Litmus paper is an indicator that changes colour due to the pH of a solution. There are two type of litmus paper – red and blue:

- red litmus paper stays red in the presence of an acid and turns blue in the presence of an alkali
- blue litmus paper turns red in the presence of an acid and stays blue in the presence of an alkali
- both papers remain as their original colour when placed in a neutral solution, such as pure water.

▶ **2** *What colour does litmus paper turn in an acidic solution?*

The pH scale

The **pH scale** tells you how acidic or alkaline a solution is. The scale measures how many hydrogen ions (H^+) are present in a solution. The scale ranges from pH 0 – most acidic (high concentration of hydrogen ions) to pH 14 – most alkaline (only a few hydrogen ions present). Solutions with a pH of 7 are neutral.

▶ **3** *An oven cleaner has a pH of 13. Is this an acidic, neutral or alkaline product?*

Universal indicator

Universal indicator is a very useful indicator. In addition to telling you whether a solution is acidic or alkaline, it can also tell you how strong an acid or alkali is. Universal indicator is made from a number of indicators. This enables it to turn into a range of colours as the pH changes:

- acidic solutions turn universal indicator red – they have a pH less than 7
- alkaline solutions turn universal indicator blue – they have a pH greater than 7
- neutral solutions turn universal indicator green – they have a pH of 7.

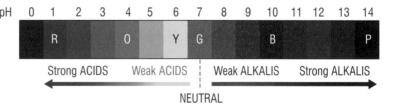

Universal indicator can be used to measure the pH of a solution

▶ **4** *What colour would universal indicator turn in lemon juice, which has a pH of 2?*

Hazard symbols

Laboratory chemicals are often labelled with **hazard symbols**. The hazard symbol shows that a potentially dangerous substance is present. The symbol has an easily recognisable image that shows you the potential hazard. Recognising this symbol allows you to minimise the chance of any danger occurring.

▷ **1** *What is a hazard symbol?*

Hazard symbols are also shown on the packaging of chemicals used in the home. For example, many cleaning products contain chemicals that could be harmful if not used correctly.

The most common hazard symbols you will encounter are shown in the table below.

Hazard symbol	Risk	Precautions	Examples of chemicals
Harmful	Can damage your health.	Do not inhale, eat or drink, or allow to come into contact with skin. If contact with skin, immediately wash well with water. Eye protection should be worn.	Sodium carbonate Copper carbonate
Irritant	Can damage skin (rashes and blisters), eyes and breathing passages.	Do not inhale, eat or drink, or allow contact with skin. If contact with skin, immediately wash well with water. Eye protection should be worn.	Dilute* solutions of all the acids and alkalis you will work with.
Corrosive	Can cause chemical burns – damages living tissue.	Wear gloves and eye protection.	Hydrochloric acid Concentrated solutions of sodium hydroxide
Flammable	Likely to catch fire.	Keep sealed and away from heat sources.	Ethanol
Toxic	Poisonous – can cause death.	Wear gloves. Do not eat or drink.	Concentrated solutions of most of the acids and alkalis you will work with.

* 'Dilute' means anything other than concentrated. All the acids and alkalis that you will work will have already been diluted.

D.13

Key points

- Indigestion remedies contain weak alkalis that neutralise excess acid in the stomach.
- Lime is added to acidic soil to make it more neutral.
- Powdered limestone can be added to lakes to reduce acidity caused by acid rain.

Exam tip

Be careful when explaining how indigestion tablets work. They do not neutralise the stomach. The stomach needs to be acidic to provide the optimum conditions for digestive enzymes to work and to kill off microorganisms.

Uses of neutralisation

Curing indigestion

Too much stomach acid can result in indigestion and heartburn. Indigestion remedies taken to cure these conditions contain weak alkalis called **antacids**. These neutralise excess acid in the stomach. This increases the pH of the stomach, relieving indigestion and heartburn.

An example of an antacid taken to help ease indigestion is sodium hydrogencarbonate.

Doses of antacids need to be carefully monitored. If you take too much, the stomach pH can rise too much. A raised pH means lower acidity, which can impair digestion to such an extent that food is not properly broken down.

Magnesium hydroxide is another common antacid used in indigestion remedies. It reacts with the hydrochloric acid present in the stomach:

hydrochloric acid + magnesium hydroxide → magnesium chloride + water

acid   +   base   →   salt   + water

⟹ **1** *What is an antacid?*

Neutralising soil

Most plants prefer to grow in neutral soil that has a pH of around 7. If soil is too acidic, farmers and gardeners add alkalis to raise the pH of the soil. Common alkalis added to the soil include calcium oxide (quicklime), chalk (calcium carbonate) or calcium hydroxide (slaked lime).

⟹ **2** *Name an alkali used to neutralise acidic soils.*

Reducing acidity in lakes

When acid rain falls into lakes it can result in the pH of the lake decreasing. If a lake becomes too acidic, fish and other aquatic organisms can no longer survive. Alkalis such as powdered limestone can be added to lakes affected in this way to increase their pH, reducing the acidity. This is known as **liming**.

⟹ **3** *What happens to a lake if it becomes too acidic?*

Key words: antacid, liming

D.14

Common chemical formulae

The **chemical formula** of a substance tells you the type and number of each atom present in a molecule. For example, the chemical formula for calcium carbonate is $CaCO_3$:

One atom of carbon
↓
One atom of calcium ⟶ $CaCO_3$ ⟵ Three atoms of oxygen

This formula tells us that calcium carbonate is a molecule, containing one calcium atom, one carbon atom and three oxygen atoms. Remember, if no number is written, this means that there is only one of this type of atom in the molecule.

A reagent is a chemical substance that is used to create a reaction in combination with some other substance. The formulae for all the reagents covered in learning aim D are listed in the table below.

> **1** *What is a reagent?*

Chemical name	Chemical formula	Atoms present in a molecule
Hydrochloric acid	HCl	1 hydrogen, 1 chlorine
Nitric acid	HNO_3	1 hydrogen, 1 nitrogen, 3 oxygen
Sulfuric acid	H_2SO_4	2 hydrogen, 1 sulfur, 4 oxygen
Copper oxide	CuO	1 copper, 1 oxygen
Zinc oxide	ZnO	1 zinc, 1 oxygen
Sodium hydroxide	NaOH	1 sodium, 1 oxygen, 1 hydrogen
Sodium carbonate	Na_2CO_3	2 sodium, 1 carbon, 3 oxygen
Copper carbonate	$CuCO_3$	1 copper, 1 carbon, 3 oxygen
Calcium carbonate	$CaCO_3$	1 calcium, 1 carbon, 3 oxygen

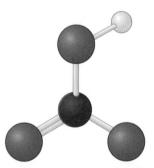

A molecule of nitric acid (HNO_3)

> **2** *What is the chemical formula for nitric acid?*

> **3** *What is the chemical name for NaOH?*

Key word: chemical formula

1 Name two indicators that can be used to determine whether a solution is an acid or an alkali.

2 **a** What is the pH of a neutral solution?

b What colour will a neutral solution turn with universal indicator?

c What colour will a neutral solution turn blue litmus paper?

3 How can you test a gas to see if it contains hydrogen?

4 **a** What does this hazard symbol stand for?

b What precautions should you take when working with a chemical labelled with this symbol?

IRRITANT

5 What salts are produced if you react magnesium with:

a hydrochloric acid   **b** sulfuric acid   **c** nitric acid?

6 Antacids are used to treat indigestion.

a Name a common compound found in an antacid.

b Explain how antacids treat indigestion.

7 Represent the reaction between sulfuric acid and zinc oxide as:

a a word equation

b a balanced chemical equation.

8 Represent the reaction between hydrochloric acid and copper carbonate as:

a a word equation

b a balanced chemical equation.

Checklist	✓ ✓ ✓
Tick when you have:	Neutralisation ☐ ☐ ☐
reviewed it after your lesson ✓ ☐ ☐	Reacting acids and metals ☐ ☐ ☐
revised once – some questions right ✓ ✓ ☐	Reacting acids and carbonates ☐ ☐ ☐
revised twice – all questions right ✓ ✓ ✓	Chemical tests for hydrogen and carbon dioxide ☐ ☐ ☐
Move on to another topic when you have all three ticks	pH tests using universal indicator and litmus ☐ ☐ ☐
	Hazard symbols ☐ ☐ ☐
	Uses of neutralisation ☐ ☐ ☐
	Common chemical formulae ☐ ☐ ☐

1 All substances are made of atoms. Sometimes these atoms combine together to form new substances.

  a Match the term to its correct definition by drawing **one** line between each term and its definition. *(3 marks)*

Element		Contains more than one type of atom bonded together
Compound		Contains only one type of atom
Mixture		Contains more than one type of element or compound

The chemical formula for carbon dioxide is CO_2.

  b i Is carbon dioxide an element or a compound? *(1 mark)*

    ii How many atoms, and of which type, make up one molecule of carbon dioxide? *(2 marks)*

2 When working with chemicals you must pay attention to the hazard symbols found on their containers. Four hazard symbols are shown below:

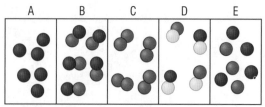

  a i Which symbol means harmful? *(1 mark)*

    ii Which symbol means corrosive? *(1 mark)*

    iii What does symbol B mean? *(1 mark)*

  b What safety precautions should you take when working with a chemical marked with symbol C? *(2 marks)*

  c Some household cleaners can damage skin, resulting in rashes and blisters. With which symbol should a chemical of this type be labelled? *(1 mark)*

3 The diagram below shows the atoms in five different substances:

  a i Name a diagram which represents a compound. Give **one** reason for your answer. *(2 marks)*

    ii Name a diagram which represents a mixture. Give **one** reason for your answer. *(2 marks)*

    iii What does diagram C represent? *(1 mark)*

  b i Which diagram could represent copper. Give **one** reason for your answer. *(2 marks)*

    ii Which diagram could represent nitrogen (N_2). Give **one** reason for your answer. *(2 marks)*

  c Draw a diagram to represent an atom of iron oxide (Fe_2O_3). *(2 marks)*

Exam tip

Look carefully at the picture on a hazard symbol – they often give you a clue to the possible risk of using this chemical. For example, a corrosive symbol shows the chemical 'eating away' at a surface and a human hand.

Exam tip

Atomic diagrams like the one in question 3 can appear confusing. Remember each atom is represented by one dot. If the dots are the same colour, they represent the same type of atom. If the dots are touching this represents that they are chemically bonded together.

4 Table salt (sodium chloride) can be made by reacting hydrochloric acid with sodium carbonate.

    a i Which of the chemicals above is an acid? *(1 mark)*

    ii When tested, what colour would this acid turn blue litmus paper? *(1 mark)*

    iii Which of the chemicals above is a base? *(1 mark)*

    b Complete the following generalised word equation for this reaction:

    acid + carbonate → salt + carbon dioxide + ... *(1 mark)*

    c Explain how you would test that carbon dioxide gas has been given off by this reaction. *(2 marks)*

5 A range of salts can be made from reacting acids with metals.

    a i What is the general word equation that can be used to represent this reaction? *(2 marks)*

    ii Explain how you would test for the gas that is given off in part **ai**. *(1 mark)*

    b Name the salt produced when aluminium reacts with sulfuric acid. *(1 mark)*

    c Zinc chloride has the chemical formula $ZnCl_2$. Write a balanced equation to represent this reaction. *(3 marks)*

    d Why should you never react Group 1 metals with acids? *(2 marks)*

6 As a result of the effects of acid rain, some lakes have become too acidic for fish to live in them. In some areas, powdered limestone (calcium carbonate) is added to lakes to remove the acidity. This process is known as liming.

    a i How could universal indicator be used to show that the reaction has been successful? *(2 marks)*

    ii What pH will the lake be once the reaction is completed? *(1 mark)*

    iii What is the difference between a base and an alkali? *(1 mark)*

    b i Write a word equation for the reaction between calcium carbonate and hydrochloric acid. *(3 marks)*

    ii Write a balanced chemical equation for the reaction between calcium carbonate and hydrochloric acid. *(3 marks)*

    c State and explain why farmers add lime to some soils. *(2 marks)*

Exam tip

When balancing an equation, begin by writing out the word equation. Then write the formula for each of the substances. Finally check that you have the same number of each type of atom in the products as you have in the reactants. This may take a couple of attempts.

Exam tip

As a rough guide, a third of the time you have available should be spent on answering the questions in the chemistry section. You have one hour to complete this exam, so spend about 20 minutes on this section of the paper.

E.1

Forms of energy and their uses

Energy is needed to make things work. There are six different forms of energy.

Thermal

Thermal energy is also known as heat energy. It is gained when the particles of a substance absorb energy. For example, constantly rubbing a piece of sandpaper over wood causes the wood to heat up.

Thermal energy is used for:

- heating – for example, in central heating systems
- cooking – for example, barbecuing food
- seeing in darkness – 'night vision', for example, it is used by the police to track suspects at night.

▶ **1** *Name three uses of thermal energy.*

Thermal imaging is used for police surveillance

Electrical

Electrical energy is produced from a range of resources. These include using fossil fuels, the wind, waves and tides. Electrical energy is easy to generate and transmit long distances. It is used to supply energy to a wide range of devices.

Electrical energy is used for:

- the energy supply for a range of domestic appliances – for example, for an iron and a microwave
- producing movement – for example, in electrically-powered cars and trains
- producing light – for example, in an energy-saving light bulb.

▶ **2** *Name three uses of electrical energy.*

Electrical energy can be used to produce movement. The French TGV train can achieve speeds of more than 500 km/h

Light

Light energy is emitted by **luminous** objects, and is reflected from coloured or shiny surfaces.

Light energy is used for:

- seeing
- generating electricity – through using solar cells
- producing and projecting images – for example, producing the image on a mobile phone screen.

▶ **3** *Name three uses of light energy.*

Solar panels are used to convert light energy directly into electrical energy

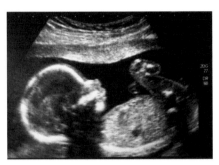

An image of an unborn baby can be produced using ultrasound waves

Sound

Sound energy is produced by objects which vibrate. Some sound frequencies are above the human hearing range – these are known as **ultrasound**.

Sound energy is used for:

- hearing and communication
- medical procedures – for example, scanning an unborn foetus
- entertainment, such as a music concert.

> **4** *Name three uses of sound energy.*

Mechanical

Mechanical energy includes potential energy and kinetic energy forms. **Potential energy** is also known as stored energy. **Kinetic energy** is also known as movement energy.

Mechanical energy is used to:

- provide movement – for example, when a roller coaster car falls quickly
- produce large forces – for example, in a pile driver
- keep energy stored for later use – for example, in water stored in a reservoir behind a dam wall.

> **5** *Name three uses of mechanical energy*

A pile driver is used to hammer building foundations into the ground

Nuclear

Nuclear energy is the energy locked up in the **nucleus** of an atom. Huge amounts of energy can be released by nuclear fission, but it needs to be carefully controlled.

Nuclear energy is used to:

- generate electricity in a nuclear power station
- release vast amounts of thermal energy in a nuclear explosion
- provide an energy supply for surgical implants, such as heart pacemakers.

> **6** *Name three uses of nuclear energy.*

Nuclear power stations produce vast supplies of electrical energy from small quantities of fuel

Key words: thermal, luminous, ultrasound, potential energy, kinetic energy, nucleus

Bump up your grade

All forms of energy can be classified as thermal, electrical, light, sound, mechanical or nuclear. Use a mnemonic to help you remember all six forms, such as:

This	Thermal
Elephant	Electrical
Loves	Light
Stealing	Sound
Monkey	Mechanical
Nuts	Nuclear

E.2

Key points

- There are six different energy stores – chemical, kinetic, gravitational potential, elastic potential, thermal and nuclear.
- Stored energy is also known as potential energy.

When natural gas (methane) is burnt, it releases heat energy

Bump up your grade

Gravitational potential energy is the energy an object has due to its position within a gravitational field. To raise an object higher, you would need to supply it with energy – so its store of gravitational energy would increase.

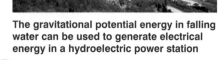

The gravitational potential energy in falling water can be used to generate electrical energy in a hydroelectric power station

Energy stores and their uses

Some forms of energy can be stored within an object and then used later. These forms of energy are known as **energy stores**. There are six different energy stores.

Chemical

When chemical reactions are used to form new substances, **chemical bonds** are created. This process often releases energy. So some chemicals can be thought of as stores of energy – chemical reactions are used to release this energy.

Chemical energy stores are used for:

- batteries – to supply electrical energy
- combustion – to supply thermal energy
- fuel cells – to supply electrical energy from fuels.

⟩⟩⟩ **1** *Name a store of chemical energy and its use.*

Kinetic

When an object is in motion, it possesses kinetic energy. This can be harnessed to produce useful forms of energy.

Kinetic energy is involved with:

- wind turbines – to harness the kinetic energy in the wind
- producing sounds – for example, when an object is caused to vibrate
- generators – converting movement into electrical energy.

⟩⟩⟩ **2** *Name a store of kinetic energy and its use.*

Wind turbines harness the power of the wind to produce electrical energy

Gravitational potential

Gravitational potential energy is stored in an object that has been raised up above ground level. You would have lots of gravitational potential energy if you stood at the top of the Eiffel tower!

Gravitational potential energy stores are used for:

- producing movement – for example, when a roller coaster makes a drop
- generating electricity – harvesting the energy from falling water
- mechanical power sources – for example, the pendulum of a clock.

⟩⟩⟩ **3** *Name a store of gravitational potential energy, and its use.*

A bungee rope stores elastic potential energy when it is stretched. This provides a force on the bungee jumper, returning them back towards their original position.

Barbecuing uses heat energy to enable a chemical reaction – cooking – to occur

Elastic potential

Elastic potential energy is the energy stored in an object that has been stretched or compressed from its original shape.

Elastic potential energy stores are used for:

● producing motion – for example, in a catapult

● providing an energy source – for example, in a wind-up toy

● providing a force to return an object towards its original position – for example, in a car suspension system.

▷ **4** *Name a store of elastic potential energy and its use.*

Thermal

Objects that have been heated contain thermal energy. This store of energy can be used in a number of ways:

● to provide movement – for example, convection currents in the oceans

● to produce electrical energy – geothermal power stations use thermal energy stored underground

● to enable chemical reactions – such as cooking food.

▷ **5** *Name a store of thermal energy and its use.*

Nuclear

A store of nuclear energy can release a lot of energy very quickly, or a smaller amount of energy over a long period of time. Both **nuclear decay** and **nuclear fission** can be used to harness nuclear energy.

Nuclear energy stores are used to:

● generate electricity in nuclear power stations

● provide a long-term power source for large ships, such as aircraft carriers

● provide a stable energy supply to remote objects – for example, satellites that explore distant planets in the Solar System.

▷ **6** *Name a store of nuclear energy and its use.*

A nuclear aircraft carrier can stay at sea for many months, without any need to refuel. Nuclear reactors provide the power source for the carrier.

Key words: energy store, chemical bonds, chemical energy, gravitational potential energy, elastic potential energy, nuclear decay, nuclear fission

E.3

A large force is needed to pull the lorry. This means a lot of energy will be required to move it through the distance of the course.

Energy transfers

Energy can be transferred between objects, and from one place to another. There are five different ways in which this can occur.

Mechanically

When a force is applied to an object, and the object moves as a result, energy is transferred. The amount of energy transferred is called the **work done**. We can say that work is done when a force moves through a distance.

The more force that is applied, or the greater the distance travelled, the more energy is transferred.

 1 *What are the two factors that affect how much energy is transferred mechanically?*

Electrically

Electrical energy is used to provide the energy for many appliances and devices in the home. As a society, we have come to rely upon electrical energy – can you imagine life without TVs, computers and mobile phones?

One advantage of using electrical energy is that it can be generated in a power station in one location and then transferred easily over long distances. The **National Grid** power distribution system transfers electrical energy across the country. Within a house, electrical energy is transferred using the household wiring system – usually on a circuit called a **ring main**.

The National Grid is used to transfer electrical energy around the UK

 2 *Give one reason why electrical energy is so useful.*

Conduction

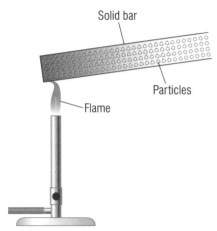

Energy transfer in a solid. Vibrations are passed from particle to particle.

Thermal energy can be transferred through a material by **conduction**. Solids are better **conductors** than liquids. Metals are the best thermal conductors of all. Gases are the best thermal **insulators**.

Conduction always occurs **from** warmer places **to** cooler places.

Conduction works in the following way:

In a solid, the particles vibrate in fixed positions. When thermal energy is added, the particles gain kinetic energy and so vibrate more. This makes these particles collide with other particles, which passes the energy along. The thermal energy is transferred through the material.

▷ **3** *List the following materials in order, from best conductor to worst conductor: liquid, gas, non-metal, metal.*

Convection

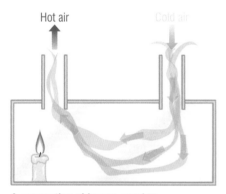

A convection chimney, used to demonstrate convection currents

The particles in a liquid or a gas are free to move around – we call them **fluids**. Thermal energy can be transferred through a fluid by convection. This process causes the particles in the fluid to move, transferring energy with them.

Hot fluids rise and colder fluids sink. The resulting movement of the fluid is called a **convection current**.

Convection occurs because the particles in a fluid spread out when heated. This makes a hot fluid less **dense**, so it 'floats' up on top of a cooler, more dense fluid. Colder fluids are denser, so they sink down below the warmer parts of the fluid.

▷ **4** *What is meant by a convection current?*

Radiation

Radiation is the energy that is given out by an object. Hot objects emit infrared radiation. This radiation:
● travels in straight lines away from the hot object
● is emitted in all directions
● is transferred from hotter places to colder places.

The rate of energy transfer depends on the difference in temperature between the object and its surroundings. The greater the temperature difference, the more infrared radiation will be emitted.

Dark surfaces are good absorbers and emitters of infrared radiation. Pale surfaces are good reflectors and poor emitters of infrared radiation.

Vibrating objects also emit a form of radiation – sound energy. This is transferred by sound waves from one place to another.

▷ **5** *Does infrared energy move from hot to cold regions, or from cold places to hot places?*

> ### Exam tip
> When describing why convection occurs, remember it is a hot fluid that rises. It is not correct to say 'heat rises'.

> ### Exam tip
> Remember that dark surfaces are good at absorbing infrared radiation AND emitting it.

Key words: work done, National Grid, ring main, conduction, conductor, insulator, fluid, convection current, dense, radiation

1 What are the six forms of energy?

2 Name the six stores of energy.

3 List five ways energy can be transferred from one place to another.

4 What is gravitational potential energy?

5 Which store of energy would be found in a spring which has been compressed?

6 What is meant by 'mechanical energy'?

7 What are the three ways in which thermal energy can be transferred?

8 Why do convection currents occur in fluids, but not in solids?

9 Explain how energy is released from a chemical store of energy.

10 Give one reason why nuclear fuels are used to generate electricity.

11 Explain how convection currents are formed.

Checklist ✓ ✓ ✓

Tick when you have:				Forms of energy and their uses			
reviewed it after your lesson	✓	☐	☐		☐	☐	☐
revised once – some questions right	✓	✓	☐	Energy stores and their uses	☐	☐	☐
revised twice – all questions right	✓	✓	✓		☐	☐	☐
Move on to another topic when you have all three ticks				Energy transfers	☐	☐	☐

E.4ab

Key points

- Energy is measured in joules (J).
- Energy cannot be created or destroyed, only transferred from one form to another.
- Energy transfer diagrams can be used to show how energy is transferred from one form to another.

Light bulbs convert electrical energy into light energy (useful) and thermal energy (wasted). The thermal energy is dissipated into the atmosphere.

Roller coasters convert gravitational potential energy into kinetic energy

Bump up your grade

Remember that all energy transfers will produce thermal energy. This is often wasted energy, because the thermal energy is too dilute to be made use of.

Energy transfer – the conservation of energy

Energy is measured in **joules** (J). The energy required to lift a weight of 1 **newton** through a distance of 1 metre is 1 joule. This is roughly the energy needed to lift an apple from the floor, up to a kitchen worktop height.

Larger quantities of energy are often measured in kJ (kilojoules – 1 kJ = 1000 J) or MJ (megajoules – 1 MJ = 1 000 000 J).

▶ **1** *What is meant by a kilojoule?*

The law of conservation of energy

The **law of conservation of energy** states that energy cannot be created or destroyed, only transferred from one form to another.

All forms of energy eventually end up in the form of thermal energy. When energy becomes too spread out ('diluted') to be useful, we say the energy has been **dissipated**.

▶ **2** *What is the law of conservation of energy?*

Energy transfer equations

When energy is transferred from one form to another, the transfer can be represented using an energy transfer equation.

For example, a light bulb transfers electrical energy (the energy supply) into light energy (what we want – **useful energy**) and thermal energy (energy we don't want – **wasted energy**). This is represented as:

electrical energy → **light energy** + **thermal energy**
(energy supply) → (useful energy) + (wasted energy)

When a roller coaster car descends, the kinetic energy it gains comes from the gravitational potential energy it had from being high up:

gravitational potential energy → **kinetic energy** + **thermal energy** + **sound energy**
(energy supply) → (useful energy) + (wasted energy)

Thermal energy is always produced in an energy transfer, due to friction or electrical heating. This is often too dilute to be useful, and so it is dissipated into the atmosphere.

▶ **3** *When an energy transfer occurs, what is the name given to the forms of energy created which we do not want?*

Exam tip

If an exam question asks you to describe the energy transfers that are taking place in a device, use an energy transfer equation as part of your answer. This makes it very clear that you understand which forms of energy are involved. It is worth practising these equations for a range of devices.

Key words: joule, newton, law of conservation of energy, dissipate, useful energy, wasted energy

E.4c

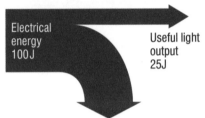

A Sankey diagram to represent the energy transfer in a light bulb

Energy transfer – Sankey diagrams

Due to the law of conservation of energy, the total energy given out from a device is always equal to the total energy that is supplied to the device.

For example, if we supply 100 J of energy to a light bulb, it produces 25 J of light energy and 75 J of heat energy:

electrical energy → light energy + thermal energy
100 J → 25 J + 75 J

▶ **1** *Which form of 'wasted' energy is produced by a light bulb?*

Sankey diagrams

A **Sankey diagram** is a scale drawing used to represent an energy transfer. It can be used to work out how much useful, or wasted, energy a device produces.

▶ **2** *What is a Sankey diagram?*

Maths skills – Constructing Sankey diagrams

Sankey diagrams should be drawn to scale, using graph paper. The width of the arrow used represents the quantity of energy. Look at the worked example below. A radio uses 130 J of electrical energy per second. It produces 40 J of sound energy and 90 J of thermal energy. Construct a Sankey diagram to represent this change.

Step 1 – Write down the energy transfer equation:

electrical energy → sound energy + thermal energy

Step 2 – Choose a scale, which will allow your largest arrow to fit on the graph paper. In this case, we will choose 1 square = 10 J.

Step 3 – Draw the input energy and useful and wasted form(s) of energy to scale.

Scale: 1 square = 10 J

Electrical input energy is 130 J = 13 squares in scale.

Sound energy output is 40 J = 4 squares in scale.

Wasted thermal energy output is 90 J = 9 squares in scale.

Scale: 1 square = 10 J

Sound energy

Input: Electrical energy

Thermal energy

▶ **3** *How would the Sankey diagram for a radio look different if it produced more sound energy for the same amount of input energy?*

E.4de

Key points

- Power is measured in watts (W) or kilowatts (kW).
- Power is the rate of energy transfer.
- Power = $\dfrac{\text{energy transferred}}{\text{time}}$.

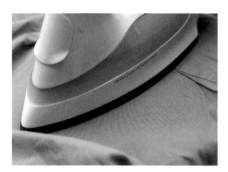

An iron transfers electrical energy into thermal energy. A typical power rating for an iron is 2 kW.

Bump up your grade

Physics equations always require you to work in standard units. Examples are: m, s, J and W. Make sure that you convert a non-standard unit, for example, 1 minute = 60 s.

Exam tip

Don't forget to add units to a numerical answer – this is often worth a mark in an exam.

At the end of the exam paper, it is good practice to check that you have added the correct units to your answers.

Key word: power

Energy transfer – power

Power

Power is the rate of energy transfer. This means it is a measure of how much energy is transferred per second. It is measured in watts (W) or kilowatts (kW), where 1 kW = 1000 W.

When 1 joule of energy is transferred in 1 second, the power will be 1 W. So we can say that a rate of energy transfer (power) of 1 joule per second (J/s) is 1 W. For example, a 60 W light bulb transfers 60 J of electrical energy to light and heat energy per second.

➡ **1** *What is power?*

➡ **2** *How many watts are there in 3 kilowatts?*

The more powerful a device is, the faster the rate at which it will transfer energy. Some typical power ratings of household devices are shown below:

Device	Power rating
Light bulb	60 W
TV	100 W
Hairdryer	2500 W (2.5 kW)
Electric shower	9000 W (9 kW)

Electrical devices that are designed to produce a heating effect tend to have a higher power rating than other devices.

Maths skills – Calculating power

To calculate power, use the following equation:

$$\text{Power (W)} = \frac{\text{energy transferred (J)}}{\text{time (s)}}$$

This can be learnt as an equation triangle:

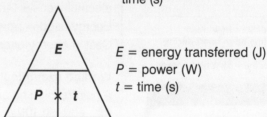

E = energy transferred (J)
P = power (W)
t = time (s)

Worked example 1

If 100 joules of energy are required to lift an object, and the process takes 5 seconds, the power required would be:

$$\text{power} = \frac{\text{energy transferred}}{\text{time}} = \frac{100}{5} = \mathbf{20\,W}$$

Worked example 2

How much energy will be transferred by a 60 W light bulb in 3 minutes?

$$\text{Energy} = \text{power} \times \text{time} = 60 \times 180 = \mathbf{10\,800\,J}$$

➡ **3** *How much energy is transferred when a 750 W vacuum cleaner is used for 10 minutes?*

E.4f

Energy transfer – the cost of electricity

Measuring domestic electrical energy

Every home in the UK has an electricity meter. It measures how much electrical energy the household uses. The more devices that the household uses, and the longer they are used for, the more energy is used.

The amount of energy used is measured in **kilowatt-hours** (kWh). 1 kilowatt-hour is the amount of energy that is transferred from electrical energy to other forms, when a device of power rating 1 kW (1000 W) is switched on for 1 hour (3600 s).

▷ **1** *What is a kilowatt-hour?*

Units of electricity

An electricity bill tells you how many 'units' of electricity you have used.

$$1 \text{ unit} = 1 \text{ kWh}$$

So, in effect, an electricity bill is telling you how many kWh of energy have been used in your household.

▷ **2** *What is a 'unit' of electricity?*

Key points

- An electricity meter in your home measures how much electrical energy has been used.
- Electrical power used in your home is measured in kilowatt-hours.
- 1 kWh = 1 unit of electricity.

A typical domestic electricity meter

L. Jones
26 Homewood Road
Otwood M51 9YZ

Meter readings present	Meter readings previous	units	pence per unit	amount	VAT %
31534	30092	1442	10.89	157.03	Zero
Standing charge				17.30	
TOTAL NOW DUE				174.33	
PERIOD ENDED				31.03.10	

**Electricity bills measure how much electrical energy has been used during the billing period.
One unit of electricity = 1 kWh of energy.**

Exam tip

Ensure that you set out your working for a calculation question clearly. Follow the same approach each time:

1 Write down the equation being used.
2 Substitute in the values.
3 Write down the answer.
4 Include the unit with your answer.

Remember to be careful with pounds and pence; 14p is £0.14.

📟 **Maths skills – Calculating the cost of electricity**

The cost of using an electrical device can be calculated using the following two formulae:

$$\text{energy used (units)} = \text{power (kW)} \times \text{time (hours)}$$
$$\text{cost of electricity} = \text{energy used (units)} \times \text{cost per unit (p)}$$

Worked example 1

How much does it cost to use a 2 kW electric fire for 4 hours? Each unit of electricity costs 14p.

Energy used = power (kW) × time (hours) = 2 × 4 = 8 units
Cost = energy used × cost per unit = 8 × 14 = 112p = **£1.12**

Worked example 2

A hairdressing salon uses four 3 kW hairdryers for an average of 4½ hours per day, and ten 100 W light bulbs, for an average of 6 hours per day. What will the electricity bill be for the salon for one day, if electricity costs 12p per kWh?

Hairdryers: energy used = power (kW) × time (hours) = (4 × 3) × 4.5 = 54 units
Light bulbs: energy used = power (kW) × time (hours) = (10 × 0.1) × 6 = 6 units
Total energy used = 60 units (= 60 kWh)
Cost = energy used × cost per unit = 60 × 12 = 720p = **£7.20**

▷ **3** *How much would a 150 W computer cost to use for 1– 2 hours, at a cost per unit of 15p?*

Key words: kilowatt-hour, unit (of electricity)

E.5

Efficiency

The energy a device transfers, which it is designed to produce, is known as the **useful energy**. For example, the useful energy output from a TV would be light energy and sound energy.

All devices, no matter how well they are designed, also transfer energy into forms we do not want. This is known as **wasted energy**. For example, a TV also produces thermal energy.

Energy transfer diagram for a TV:

electrical energy → light energy + sound energy + thermal energy
energy supply **useful energy** **useful energy** **wasted energy**

➤ **1** *What is meant by 'useful' energy?*

Efficiency

Efficiency measures how well a device does its job. An efficient device transfers most of the energy supply into useful forms of energy. This means that little wasted energy will be produced.

Efficiency is measured as a percentage. So, if a device is 60% efficient, it would convert 60% of the energy supplied to it into useful forms. This means that 40% of the energy supplied to it would be wasted.

➤ **2** *What does efficiency measure?*

Maths skills – Efficiency

To calculate the efficiency of a device, use the following equation:
$$\text{efficiency (\%)} = \frac{\text{useful energy output}}{\text{total energy input}} \times 100$$

Worked example 1

An electric motor produces 125 J of useful work. Calculate its efficiency if it was supplied with 500 J of electrical energy.

$$\text{Efficiency (\%)} = \frac{\text{useful energy output}}{\text{total energy input}} \times 100 = \frac{125}{500} \times 100 = \mathbf{25\%}$$

Worked example 2

How much useful light energy would be produced by an 'energy-saving' light bulb which is 25% efficient, and has been supplied with 300 J of electrical energy?

$$\frac{\text{useful energy output}}{\text{total energy input}} \times 100 = \text{efficiency (\%)}$$

$$\frac{\text{useful energy output}}{300} \times 100 = \frac{25}{100}$$

$$\frac{\text{useful energy output}}{300} = 0.25$$

$$\text{useful energy output} = 0.25 \times 300 = \mathbf{75\,J}$$

➤ **3** *What is the equation for calculating the efficiency of a device?*

E.6a

Sources and storage of energy – renewable

Electricity can be generated in many different ways. Each method of producing electricity is known as an **energy source**. Sources of energy which will never run out are known as **renewable** energy sources.

 1 *What is a renewable energy source?*

Solar energy

Solar cells convert light directly into electrical energy. Solar panels can be fitted to a roof to provide free electricity to the homeowner.

- Advantages – no running costs, can be used in remote locations.
- Disadvantages – expensive to buy, only work in the daytime, may only produce a small amount of power.

 **2** *Name an advantage and a disadvantage of solar power.*

Wind energy

Wind turbines convert kinetic energy in the wind into electrical energy. To produce a large amount of power, many wind turbines need to be used in an area – this is known as a wind farm.

- Advantages – produce no greenhouse gases or acid rain, simple technology.
- Disadvantages – noisy, cannot be used if wind speed is too low or too high, unsightly.

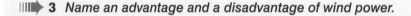 **3** *Name an advantage and a disadvantage of wind power.*

Biofuels

Fuels, which are produced from living, or recently living, material are known as **biofuels**. Examples of biofuels include:

- methane – obtained from decaying rubbish and sewage works
- wood – from trees
- ethanol – from fermenting sugar cane.

Biofuels are burnt. The heat produced converts water into steam. Steam is used to turn turbines. Turbines turn generators, which produce electricity.

- Advantages – convert stored energy in waste products into useful electrical energy, **carbon neutral** (in other words, the carbon released by burning the waste originally came from the atmosphere anyway).
- Disadvantages – large areas of land are required to grow biofuels, fuel needs to be transported from where it is grown to the biofuel power station.

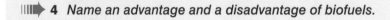 **4** *Name an advantage and a disadvantage of biofuels.*

Large areas of land are required to grow biofuels. In some countries, large-scale deforestation has taken place to create space to grow these crops.

Hydroelectric power

Rain water can be collected in a reservoir – a large, artificial lake. When it is allowed to flow downhill, the water spins turbines, which turn generators, which produce electricity.

- Advantages – reliable, requires no fuel source, reservoir provides a location for leisure and sporting activities.
- Disadvantages – land must be flooded to produce a reservoir, can only be used in hilly locations.

River valleys must be flooded to produce a hydroelectric scheme

Wave power

When waves pass a point in the sea, they cause the surface to move up and down. This movement causes machinery to move, turning a generator. The generator converts kinetic energy into electrical energy.

- Advantages – produces no greenhouse gases, cheap and simple to operate.
- Disadvantages – do not produce a constant supply of electricity, buildings and cabling can spoil coastlines.

▶ **5** *Name an advantage and a disadvantage of wave power.*

Tidal power

Tidal power stations trap water from a high tide behind a barrier, known as a tidal barrage. The water is then released – as it flows, it turns turbines, which turn generators, which produce electricity.

- Advantages – reliable, produce no polluting gases to the atmosphere.
- Disadvantages – can only be built in a limited number of locations, habitats are affected in the area surrounding the barrage, electricity is only produced when tides are going in or out.

Tidal barrages can produce large amounts of electrical energy, but there are few locations worldwide where they can be built

Geothermal energy

The thermal energy stored in hot rocks underground can be used to produce electricity. Cold water is pumped into the hot rocks and it returns as steam. The steam is then used to turn turbines, which turn generators, which produce electricity.

- Advantages – no fuel source is required, little space is required for a geothermal power station.
- Disadvantages – harmful and polluting gases can be released from deep underground, can only be used in locations where hot rocks exist underground.

▶ **6** *Name an advantage and a disadvantage of geothermal energy.*

> **Exam tip**
>
> A renewable source of energy is one which will never run out. This does not mean that it can be used again – this is recyclable. Ensure that you have the correct definition and do not mix up these two terms.

Key words: energy source, renewable, biofuel, carbon neutral

E.6b

Key points

- Non-renewable energy sources will run out in the future.
- Fossil fuels are coal, oil and natural gas.
- The non-renewable energy sources are coal, oil, natural gas and nuclear.

Sources and storage of energy – non-renewable

Over 90% of the electricity needed in the UK is generated using **fossil fuels** or nuclear power. Fossil fuels are coal, oil and natural gas. All of these sources will run out in the future – this means they are **non-renewable**.

▶ **1** *What is meant by a non-renewable energy source?*

Fossil fuels

Around three quarters of the UK's electricity is generated using fossil fuels. All fossil fuel based power stations work in the same way.

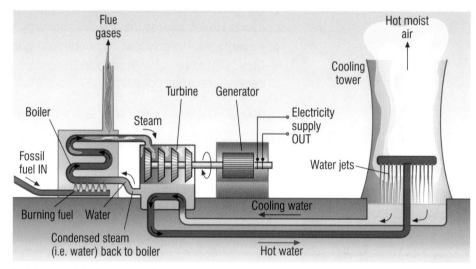

Inside a fossil fuel power station

- The fossil fuel is burnt. This transfers chemical energy in the fuel into thermal energy.
- The thermal energy boils water, converting it to steam.
- Steam drives turbines.
- The turbines are connected to a generator. When the turbines spin, so does the generator.
- The generator converts kinetic energy into electrical energy.

Each fossil fuel has advantages and disadvantages to its use. These are:

Fossil fuel	% of UK electricity generation	Advantages	Disadvantages
Coal	30	Reliable Widely available Cheap	Difficult to transport Releases carbon dioxide and sulfur dioxide when burnt
Oil	1	Reliable Easy to transport	Releases carbon dioxide and sulfur dioxide when burnt
Natural gas	45	Reliable Most efficient fossil fuel Easy to transport	Releases carbon dioxide when burnt

▶ **2** *Name an advantage, and a disadvantage, for each of the fossil fuels.*

All fossil fuels release carbon dioxide when burnt. This adds to the greenhouse effect, causing global warming. Burning coal and oil also releases sulfur dioxide – the gas which causes acid rain.

Nuclear power

Around 13% of our electricity is generated in nuclear power stations. These work by harnessing the thermal energy released during **nuclear fission**. Otherwise, these power stations work in the same way as a conventional fossil fuel power station.

Nuclear fuels have several advantages over fossil fuels:

- no carbon dioxide is released – so they do not contribute to global warming
- no sulfur dioxide is released – so they do not add to the problem of acid rain
- uranium (nuclear fuel) has a very high energy density – so much less fuel is needed
- uranium reserves are estimated at around 200 years.

However, there are also significant disadvantages to using nuclear power:

- radioactive waste is produced from nuclear fission, which is harmful to health. It needs storing safely for many thousands of years
- if a nuclear accident occurred, it would make the region around the nuclear reactor uninhabitable for many years
- shutting down (decommissioning) a nuclear reactor at the end of its life costs billions of pounds.

⟱▶ **3** *State an advantage, and a disadvantage, of using nuclear power.*

Key words: fossil fuels, non-renewable, nuclear fission

E.6c

Sources and storage of energy – using energy stores effectively

All of the **non-renewable** sources of energy will run out in the future. It is important that we use these sources as effectively as possible. Scientists and engineers are taking steps to ensure that supplies of fossil fuels, and nuclear fuel, last as long as possible. These include:

- Producing the right amount of electricity. Electrical energy cannot be stored, so it is important that not too much electricity is generated.
- Improving the **efficiency** of power stations. Modern gas-fired power stations are around 50% efficient, compared with around 33% for coal-fired and oil-fired power stations.
- Making greater use of renewable resources. This will conserve fossil fuels for the future.
- Encouraging homes and businesses to be more energy efficient. The less electrical energy required by consumers, the less needs to be generated – so fewer fossil fuels are needed.

⟱▶ **1** *State one step which can be taken to use energy stores as effectively as possible.*

Key words: non-renewable, efficiency

E.6d

Sources and storage of energy – storage of energy

The key disadvantage of using electrical energy is that it cannot be stored in large quantities. If it is not used it is wasted. Batteries and fuel cells allow small amounts of energy to be stored, so that it can be transferred later. They also allow devices that use electrical energy to be used away from the mains electricity supply for a limited time.

Batteries

A **battery** uses a chemical reaction to convert stored chemical energy into electrical energy. Car batteries, for example, use the reaction between lead and sulfuric acid to produce a 12 V output. Different chemical reactions produce different voltages. It is possible to design a battery to suit a particular need or device.

> ➤ **1** *What is a battery?*

Batteries provide a convenient means of providing power to electrical devices which cannot be plugged in. However, they have a short lifespan and need replacing regularly.

Rechargeable batteries contain chemicals which allow a **reversible reaction** to occur. When the chemical reaction occurs in one direction, electrical energy is transferred **from** the cell. By supplying electrical energy **to** the cell, the chemical reaction reverses. This means that once the reaction is complete the battery will be available to use once more.

The diagram shows a reversible chemical reaction, where chemicals A and B react to form chemicals C and D.

> ➤ **2** *What is a reversible reaction?*

Fuel cells

Fuel cells transfer stored chemical energy into electrical energy through a chemical reaction with oxygen (an **oxidation** reaction). They require a constant supply of the fuel and oxygen, to work – this makes them different to batteries. Although single-fuel cells only produce a small amount of electricity, when several fuel cells are used together, significant power can be produced.

> ➤ **3** *What is a fuel cell?*

Hydrogen is often used as the fuel. When hydrogen reacts with oxygen, water is produced. This is a fuel cell that produces no polluting gases.

Fuel cells are used in applications where a significant amount of power is required and for long periods of time. These include power systems in spacecraft, buses and ships. Several car manufacturers have plans to introduce hydrogen fuel cell vehicles over the next few years.

Key points

- Energy can be stored in batteries and fuel cells.
- Batteries and fuel cells can be used to provide power in remote locations, at any time.
- Fuel cells can provide electrical energy without producing atmospheric pollution.

If the reaction *releases* energy when it goes in this direction ...

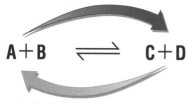

$$A + B \rightleftharpoons C + D$$

... it will *absorb* exactly the same amount of energy when it goes in this direction

Rechargeable batteries rely on reversible chemical reactions

Exam tip

Be aware of the advantages of using batteries and fuel cells to provide electrical energy. They are the only practical means of storing electrical energy for later use.

Key words: battery, reversible reaction, fuel cell, oxidation

Bump up your grade

Although hydrogen fuel cells produce no pollution in use, pollution can be created during the production of the hydrogen fuel. Energy, mostly gained from burning fossil fuels, is required to collect the hydrogen gas.

Bump up your grade

Hydrogen fuel cells provide an alternative fuel for generating electricity. However, the amount of electrical energy produced is only small – enough to power just a single vehicle. This means that fuel cells cannot be used to provide the electrical energy for a town or a city.

1 Complete the law of conservation of energy: Energy cannot be created or destroyed, only .... .

2 Name five renewable energy sources.

3 What are the units of power?

4 Other than the fossil fuels, name a non-renewable energy source.

5 State the equation used to calculate power.

6 Describe the difference between a battery and a fuel cell.

7 Why are solar power and wind power described as 'unreliable' energy sources?

8 Calculate the body power of an athlete who transfers 4500 J of energy in 5 s.

9 Explain why wasted thermal energy is always produced by a device.

10 Write a flowchart to describe the steps involved in electricity production in a nuclear power station.

11 An 'energy-saving' light bulb is 25% efficient. How much wasted thermal energy would it produce if it were supplied with 200 J of electrical energy?

Checklist ✓✓✓

Tick when you have:

reviewed it after your lesson ☑ ☐ ☐

revised once – some questions right ☑ ☑ ☐

revised twice – all questions right ☑ ☑ ☑

Move on to another topic when you have all three ticks

Energy transfer – the conservation of energy	☐	☐	☐
Energy transfer – Sankey diagrams	☐	☐	☐
Energy transfer – power	☐	☐	☐
Energy transfer – the cost of electricity	☐	☐	☐
Efficiency	☐	☐	☐
Sources and storage of energy – renewable	☐	☐	☐
Sources and storage of energy – non-renewable	☐	☐	☐
Sources and storage of energy – using energy stores effectively	☐	☐	☐
Sources and storage of energy – storage of energy	☐	☐	☐

1 a Which of the following are forms of energy? Circle the correct answers. *(2 marks)*

Kinetic   Conduction   Watt   Nuclear   Joule

b The following is an energy transfer equation for a laptop:

electrical energy → light energy + sound energy + thermal energy

i Which form of energy is the energy supply? *(1 mark)*

ii Which forms of energy are useful energy? *(2 marks)*

iii Which form of energy is wasted energy? *(1 mark)*

2 a Define the terms:

i useful energy *(1 mark)*

ii wasted energy. *(1 mark)*

b Draw an energy transfer diagram for a light bulb.
Label the useful energy and wasted energy. *(5 marks)*

c What happens to the wasted energy produced in
this energy transfer? *(1 mark)*

3 a What is meant by:

i a renewable energy source *(1 mark)*

ii a non-renewable energy source? *(1 mark)*

b Classify the following energy sources as renewable or non-renewable by
placing **one** tick in each row of the table. *(5 marks)*

Energy source	Renewable?	Non-renewable?
Coal		
Solar		
Geothermal		
Nuclear		
Wind		

4 Thermal energy can be transferred in three different ways – conduction, convection
and radiation.

Join the boxes from the type of thermal energy transfer to its most appropriate
description. Boxes may be joined once, more than once, or not at all. *(4 marks)*

	Hot fluids rise, cold fluids sink
Conduction	
	Objects which are hotter than their surroundings emit thermal energy
Convection	
	Thermal energy transfer occurs most in solids, least in gases
Radiation	
	Thermal energy transfer through a vacuum

Exam tip

Remember, there are six forms of energy – thermal, electrical, light, sound, mechanical and nuclear. Mechanical energy can be further divided into kinetic energy and potential energy.

Exam tip

When writing an energy transfer diagram, always follow the same approach: energy supply → useful energy + wasted energy. Remember, there may be several different forms of useful and wasted energy.

Exam tip

The word 'renewable' is **not** the same as the word 'recyclable'! One of the most common exam errors is to write that 'renewable energy can be used again'. It cannot – this would mean the energy source could be recycled. Renewable energy is defined as an energy source that will never run out, if replenished, such as the wind or the tides.

5 Thermal energy can be transferred through a fluid by convection.

a What is meant by a fluid? (*1 mark*)

b Describe simply how thermal energy is transferred through a fluid by the process of convection. (*1 mark*)

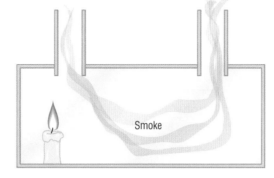

c The diagram shows the movement of air and smoke in a 'convection chimney':

i Add **three** arrows to the diagram to show the movement of air and smoke through the chimney. (*2 marks*)

ii Explain why the air moves through the chimney. (*3 marks*)

6 The diagram shows a Sankey diagram for an electric motor:

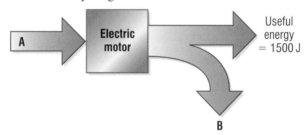

The motor is designed to lift heavy objects. If it is supplied with 6000 J of electrical energy.

a Calculate how much energy is wasted by the motor. (*1 mark*)

$$\text{Efficiency} = \frac{\text{useful energy output}}{\text{total energy input}} \times 100\%.$$

b Calculate the efficiency of the motor. (*2 marks*)

$$\text{Power} = \frac{\text{energy}}{\text{time}}.$$

c If the motor lifts the load in 6 s, calculate the power rating of the motor, stating an appropriate unit. (*3 marks*)

7 A homeowner wishes to buy new light bulbs for her home, but is unsure whether to opt for 'energy-saving' or LED bulbs. She collects the following information:

Type of bulb	Energy supplied (J)	Light energy output (J)	Thermal energy output (J)	Expected lifetime (hours)
'Energy-saving'	300	75	225	2000
LED	100	75	25	50000

a In one year, the 'energy-saving' bulb is expected to use 12 units of electricity. At a cost of 15p per kW h, calculate the cost of using this bulb for one year. (*2 marks*)

b What would the cost be of using the LED bulb for the same amount of time? (*3 marks*)

c An 'energy-saving' bulb costs £1. An LED bulb costs £8. Which bulb would you recommend to the homeowner? Include any appropriate calculations to justify your answer. (*6 marks*)

F.1

Wave characteristics

Waves are energy carriers. This means that they transfer energy from one place to another. Examples of waves include infrared radiation, sound energy and visible light.

All waves have parts that vibrate about a point. These vibrations are also known as **oscillations**. The parts that oscillate can be particles (for example, in sound waves) or magnetic and electric fields (in electromagnetic waves).

 1 *What is a wave?*

Wave types

Two different types of wave exist – **transverse** and **longitudinal**. Sound waves and some seismic (earthquake) waves are longitudinal. All electromagnetic waves are transverse.

Longitudinal waves oscillate in the same direction that the wave travels (propagates). This can be demonstrated using a slinky:

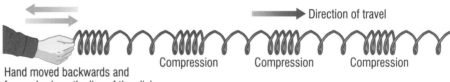

Direction of travel

Compression   Compression   Compression

Hand moved backwards and forwards along the line of the slinky

The vibrations in a longitudinal wave are parallel to the direction of wave travel

The particles of a **transverse wave** vibrate **perpendicular** to the direction that the wave travels. This can be demonstrated using a piece of rope:

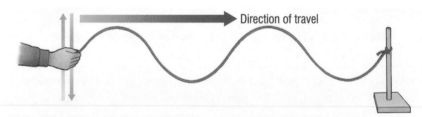

Direction of travel

The oscillations in a transverse wave are at 90° to the direction of wave travel

 2 *What are the two types of wave?*

Wave characteristics

All waves share certain things in common. For example, they all travel in straight lines. The other characteristics shared by waves include:

- they can be reflected
- they can be refracted (bent)
- they will diffract (spread out) when moving through a gap, or past an obstruction.

 3 *State three characteristics of a wave.*

Water waves can be refracted (bent) when passing from deep to shallow water

Measuring waves

Exam tip

Amplitude is measured from the peak of a wave to the mean line, or from the mean line to a trough. It is not the peak to trough distance!

All waves, whether transverse or longitudinal, are represented in the same way:

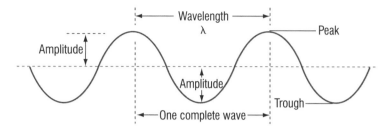

The **amplitude** of a wave is a measure of how much energy the wave is carrying. It is measured as the distance from the mean (centre) line to a peak, or from the mean line to a trough, of the wave.

Amplitude is usually measured in metres (m).

Exam tip

If you are asked to label the wavelength of a wave, ensure that your arrow goes exactly from one peak to the next, or from one trough to the next. If your labelling arrow is too short, your answer will be marked incorrect.

The **wavelength** of a wave is the distance between two identical points on the wave. This is usually measured as the distance from one peak to the next peak.

Wavelength is usually measured in metres (m).

The **frequency** of a wave is the number of waves that pass a point every second.

Frequency is measured in hertz (Hz).

1 Hz = 1 wave per second. So, if a sound wave has a frequency of 200 Hz, 200 sound waves would pass a point every second.

The **wave speed** measures the speed at which a wave travels (propagates). This can be quite fast!

Wave speed is measured in metres per second (m/s).

All electromagnetic waves travel at the **speed of light** in a vacuum (3×10^8 m/s).

4 What is meant by the amplitude of a wave?

5 What are the units of frequency?

Key words: oscillations, transverse, longitudinal, oscillate, perpendicular, amplitude, wavelength, frequency, speed of light

Bump up your grade

Make sure you learn the correct units for each quantity in a wave.
- Frequency is measured in hertz (Hz).
- Wavelength is measured in metres (m).
- Amplitude is measured in metres (m).
- Wave speed is measured in metres per second (m/s).

F.2

Wave calculations

Time period

The **frequency** of a wave is the number of waves that pass a point each second. This means that it takes a time of (1/frequency) to produce a single wave.

The time taken to produce a single wave is known as the **time period**. It is measured in seconds (s).

$$\text{Time period} = \frac{1}{\text{frequency}} \quad \text{or in symbols,} \quad T = \frac{1}{f}$$

▶ **1** *What is the time period of a wave?*

The wave equation

The speed at which a wave travels, its frequency and its wavelength are linked by the equation:

$$\text{wave speed} = \text{frequency} \times \text{wavelength}$$
$$\text{(m/s)} \qquad \text{(Hz)} \qquad \text{(m)}$$

This equation can also be written using symbols, or as an equation triangle:

$v = f \times \lambda$

v = wave speed (m/s)

f = frequency (Hz)

λ = wavelength (m)

(λ is the Greek letter lambda)

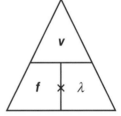

For example, if a wave has a frequency of 300 Hz, and a wavelength of 5 m, the wave speed would be:

wave speed (v) = frequency (f) × wavelength (λ) = 300 × 5 = **1500 m/s**

▶ **2** *What are the units of: a wave speed, b frequency, c wavelength?*

▶ **3** *What is the wave equation?*

Maths skills – The wave equation

Worked example

A sound wave is produced when a tuning fork vibrates 170 times per second.
a What is the frequency of the resulting sound wave?
b How long does it take to produce one oscillation?
c If the speed of sound in air is 340 m/s, what is the wavelength of the wave?

Solution

a The frequency is the number of waves produced per second = **170 Hz**

b Time to produce one wave = time period = $\dfrac{1}{\text{frequency}} = \dfrac{1}{170} = $ **0.006 s**

c From the equation triangle, wavelength, $\lambda = \dfrac{v}{f} = \dfrac{340}{170} = $ **2 m**

▶ **4** *If a wave has a time period of 20s, what is the frequency?*

Note that, for a given wave speed, if the wavelength increases the frequency decreases. The reverse is also true – if the wavelength decreases, the frequency increases. We say that frequency and wavelength are **inversely proportional** to each other.

▶ **5** *What does the term 'inversely proportional' mean?*

Using standard form

When carrying out wave calculations, you will often have to work with very large or very small numbers. It is better to express these numbers in standard form.

> ### Maths skills – Using standard form
>
> Standard form is a way of expressing a number, without using a lot of zeros. It is always written in the form: $A \times 10^n$ (where A is a number between 1 and 10, and n is an integer value). The value of n is dependent on how many times the decimal place is moved within a number.
>
> So, for example:
>
> 400000 is the same as $4 \times 10 \times 10 \times 10 \times 10 \times 10$. This would be written as 4×10^5
>
> 6230000 is the same as $6.23 \times 10 \times 10 \times 10 \times 10 \times 10 \times 10$. This would be written as 6.23×10^6
>
> $0.006 = 6 \div 10 \div 10 \div 10 = 6 \times 10^{-3}$
>
> 0.000045 is the same as $4.5 \div 10 \div 10 \div 10 \div 10 \div 10 = 4.5 \times 10^{-5}$
>
> **Worked example 1 – Converting a value to standard form**
>
> Convert the following numbers to standard form:
>
> **a** 21300000
>
> $21300000 = 2.13 \times 10 \times 10 \times 10 \times 10 \times 10 \times 10 \times 10 = \mathbf{2.13 \times 10^7}$
>
> **b** 0.00003
>
> $0.00003 = 3 \div 10 \div 10 \div 10 \div 10 \div 10 = \mathbf{3 \times 10^{-5}}$
>
> **Worked example 2 – The wave equation and standard form**
>
> An electromagnetic wave of frequency 6×10^{14} Hz has a wavelength of 5×10^{-7} m. What is the wave speed?
>
> $v = f \times \lambda = 6 \times 10^{14} \times 5 \times 10^{-7} = \mathbf{3 \times 10^8\,m/s}$
>
> **Worked example 3**
>
> An electromagnetic wave travels through glass at 2×10^8 m/s. If it has a frequency of 4×10^{11} Hz, what is its wavelength?
>
> From the equation triangle, wavelength, $\lambda = \dfrac{v}{f} = \dfrac{2 \times 10^8}{4 \times 10^{11}} = 0.0005 = \mathbf{5 \times 10^{-4}\,m}$

Bump up your grade

To enter a number into your calculator in standard form, use the EXP button. EXP means '× 10 to the power of'. So, to enter 3.5×10^{13} you would type 3.5 EXP 13 into your calculator.

Key words: frequency, time period, inversely proportional

F.3

The electromagnetic spectrum

The **electromagnetic (e.m.) spectrum** is a family of waves, all of which share very similar properties. All waves in the spectrum:

- are the oscillations of electric and magnetic fields
- do not need particles to transfer the wave from one place to another
- travel at the speed of light (3×10^8 m/s) in a **vacuum**
- can be reflected, refracted and diffracted.

▌▌▌➤ **1 What is the electromagnetic spectrum?**

Groups in the electromagnetic spectrum

The electromagnetic spectrum is continuous. However, it can be divided into different groups. Each group of waves in the electromagnetic spectrum has its own properties, which are different to the other waves in the spectrum. This is how the groups are put together. For example, radio waves can pass through the atmosphere without being completely absorbed. This makes them ideal for communications.

Because each group in the spectrum has different properties, we can use each group for different things (See F.4 Uses of waves in the electromagnetic spectrum for more detail.)

There are seven different groups of waves in the electromagnetic spectrum. These are:

- radio waves
- microwaves
- infrared
- visible light
- ultraviolet
- X-rays
- gamma rays.

▌▌▌➤ **2 What are the seven groups of waves in the electromagnetic spectrum?**

The electromagnetic spectrum is usually drawn in order from the lowest frequency through to the highest frequency wave.

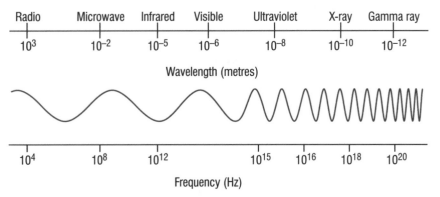

The electromagnetic spectrum, drawn in order from radio waves (longest wavelength, lowest frequency) to gamma radiation (shortest wavelength, highest frequency)

The visible spectrum contains the colours red, orange, yellow, green, blue, indigo and violet

Radio waves – wavelength: > 1 m

These waves have the longest wavelength and so the lowest frequency. This means they carry very little energy. Radio waves pass through air relatively easily. Some radio waves can reflect off a layer in the Earth's upper atmosphere, known as the ionosphere.

Microwaves – wavelength: 1 mm to 1 m

Microwaves pass easily through air and are not reflected by layers in the upper atmosphere. However, they are absorbed readily by water molecules.

▐▐▐➡ **3** *State a property of microwaves.*

Infrared – wavelength: $1\,\mu m$ to 1 mm ($1\,\mu m = 1 \times 10^{-6}\,m$)

This form of radiation is given out by objects that are hotter than their surroundings.

Visible light – wavelength: $4 \times 10^{-7}\,m$ to $7 \times 10^{-7}\,m$

These waves have the only wavelengths of the electromagnetic spectrum that our eyes are able to detect. The **visible spectrum** ranges from red light (longest wavelength) to violet light (shortest wavelength).

▐▐▐➡ **4** *What is the order of colours in the visible spectrum?*

Ultraviolet – wavelength: $10^{-9}\,m$ to $10^{-8}\,m$

Ultraviolet radiation (often shortened to 'UV radiation') reaches the Earth's surface from the Sun. It is the part of the electromagnetic spectrum that is responsible for causing skin to tan in the summer.

X-rays – wavelength: $10^{-10}\,m$ to $10^{-9}\,m$

X-rays have a wavelength that is about the same as the size of an atom – about one tenth of a billionth of a metre. X-rays can penetrate some materials.

Gamma rays – wavelength: $<10^{-10}\,m$

Gamma rays have the shortest wavelength in the electromagnetic spectrum, and so have the highest frequency. This means they transfer the most energy of any wave in the electromagnetic spectrum.

> **Key words:** electromagnetic (e.m.) spectrum, vacuum, visible spectrum

Bump up your grade

Remember, frequency is inversely proportional to wavelength. This means that long wavelength waves have a low frequency, and short wavelength waves have a high frequency.

Exam tip

You could be asked to name the missing waves from a part-completed electromagnetic spectrum. Be aware that the spectrum could be drawn in two different ways – from the longest wavelength to the shortest wavelength (radio to gamma) or highest frequency to lowest frequency (gamma to radio).

1. Which one of the following statements is correct?
   a All waves cause particles to move up and down.
   b All waves are energy carriers.
   c All waves require particles to move from one place to another.

2. At which speed do electromagnetic waves travel?

3. How many groups of waves are there in the electromagnetic spectrum?

4. Which equation links together frequency, wave speed and wavelength?

5. List the waves of the electromagnetic spectrum, in order from highest to lowest frequency.

6. Describe the difference between a longitudinal wave and a transverse wave.

7. Name three waves that can move through a vacuum.

8. The diagram shows a water wave passing a point, P.

   a Make a copy of the diagram, and label:
      i   the amplitude of the wave
      ii the wavelength of the wave.
   b Describe the motion of point P
     as the wave passes.

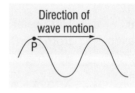

A water wave

9. Convert the following values into standard form:
   a 100   b 300 000   c 2 550 000   d 0.0003   e 0.0000067

10. A loudspeaker emits 400 sound waves every 20 seconds. If the speed of sound in air is 340 m/s, calculate:
    a the frequency of the sound waves
    b the time period of the waves
    c the wavelength of the waves.

F.4ab

Key points

- Radio waves and microwaves can pass through the Earth's atmosphere easily.
- Radio waves are used for broadcasting and satellite transmissions.
- Microwaves are used for satellite transmissions, cooking, communications and weather forecasting.

Radio waves pass through the atmosphere easily. This allows us to make radio wave observations of the Universe from ground level, using a radio telescope.

Uses of radio waves and microwaves

Radio waves and microwaves are found at the lower **frequency** end of the **electromagnetic spectrum**. This means that these waves carry little energy. They have relatively long wavelengths.

- Radio waves have wavelengths greater than 1 m.
- Microwaves have wavelengths from around 1 mm to 1 m.

Radio waves

Radio waves pass through the Earth's atmosphere easily. As they have a long wavelength, the waves diffract (spread out) as they travel around the Earth. You don't necessarily need to be in the line of sight of a radio transmitter to be able to receive the signal.

Because of these properties, radio waves are used for:

- transmitting radio and TV signals
- transmitting information from satellites towards the Earth's surface
- observations of the Universe – for example, all stars emit radio waves.

⏭ **1** *State two uses of radio waves.*

Microwaves

Microwaves pass through the Earth's atmosphere easily. As they have a higher frequency than radio waves, they carry more information. Microwaves are absorbed by water molecules and reflect off a range of different materials – metal is a particularly good reflector of microwaves.

Because of these properties, microwaves are used for:

- communications – such as military radios and mobile phone transmissions
- cooking food quickly – water molecules absorb microwave energy and heat up as a result
- radar – reflected microwaves can be used to locate an aircraft in the sky
- weather forecasting – radar measurements can provide detailed information about a cloud system, to form an accurate forecast.

⏭ **2** *State two uses of microwaves.*

Key words: frequency, electromagnetic spectrum

> ### Bump up your grade
>
> Microwaves require a line of sight to be able to communicate a signal. So, satellite transmissions from overhead are no problem. Longer wavelength radio waves are able to bend around the surface of the Earth and so are more useful for ground-based communications.

F.4cd

Thermal image of a house, showing the areas where most heat is lost (red and yellow) and areas which are well insulated (light and dark blue)

Uses of infrared and visible light

Infrared radiation is emitted from objects that are hotter than their surroundings. It can be reflected from shiny or pale surfaces and absorbed by dull, matt surfaces. Visible light is the only part of the electromagnetic spectrum that is detected by cells in our eyes – which allows us to see.

Infrared

Infrared radiation is one of the three ways thermal energy can be transferred from one place to another (see E.3 Energy transfers). Similar to light, infrared radiation can pass through transparent materials, so it will pass through air easily. However it will be absorbed or reflected when it strikes a surface.

Because of these properties, infrared radiation is used for:

- cooking – thermal energy is transferred from the cooking device to the food.
- **thermal imaging** ('night vision') – living organisms are usually warmer than their surroundings. An infrared detector can pick up this radiation and display it in the form of an image.
- **optical fibres** – information (for example, computer data) can be transmitted through an optical fibre. The infrared will travel long distances through the fibre without being absorbed.
- TV remote controls – information from a remote control is transferred to a television via infrared signals.
- security systems – many burglar alarms send an infrared signal between a transmitter and receiver. If an intruder breaks the (invisible) beam, the alarm is triggered.

1 *State two uses of infrared radiation.*

Visible light

Visible light covers the wavelengths 4×10^{-7} m to 7×10^{-7} m. Specialised cells in the retina respond to these wavelengths, sending an electrical signal to the brain. Some chemicals are affected by visible light – the energy causes a chemical reaction to occur.

Because of these properties, visible light is used for:

- vision – in humans and in many other animal species
- photography – when light strikes photographic film, it causes a permanent chemical change that represents the image which has been taken
- illumination – visible light is used to allow us to see in areas that do not have natural light, for example, when mining underground.

2 *State two uses of visible light.*

Key words: thermal imaging, optical fibre

F.4ef

Key points

- Ultraviolet and X-ray radiation are high energy electromagnetic waves.
- Ultraviolet radiation is used for fluorescent lamps, detecting forged bank notes and disinfecting water.
- X-rays are used for looking at the internal structure of objects and for medical X-rays.

Key words: frequency, fluorescent

Uses of ultraviolet and X-rays

Ultraviolet and X-ray radiation have a higher **frequency** than visible light. This means that they are high energy waves with a very short wavelength. The wavelength of X-rays is around the same size as an atom.

Ultraviolet

Ultraviolet (UV) radiation is a high energy part of the electromagnetic spectrum that is emitted naturally by the Sun. It is the ultraviolet radiation that reaches the Earth's surface which causes your skin to tan. Ultraviolet radiation can also be produced artificially, using a UV lamp. This energetic radiation can cause other atoms to fluoresce (emit light).

Because of these properties, ultraviolet radiation is used for:

- displaying ultraviolet inks – **fluorescent** lamps produce UV radiation that causes special inks to fluoresce. This is used to security mark objects – the mark is usually invisible, but will shine under a UV lamp.
- detecting forged bank notes – genuine bank notes have ultraviolet ink printed onto the paper of the note. This will become visible under a fluorescent lamp.
- disinfecting water – the energy transferred by ultraviolet radiation is large enough to kill bacteria. Therefore, potentially infected water can be disinfected by exposure to UV radiation.

⮕ **1** State two uses of ultraviolet radiation.

X-rays

X-rays are extremely high energy electromagnetic waves. They have a wavelength of between around 10^{-10} m and 10^{-9} m – a similar size to many atoms and molecules. Because they are so energetic, X-rays can penetrate and even pass through some materials, though they are absorbed by dense substances such as metals.

Because of these properties, X-rays are used for:

- studying the internal structure of materials – when X-rays are passed through a sample, atoms in the material change the direction of the X-rays. By studying the pattern produced, scientists can deduce the atomic structure of a material.
- producing medical X-ray images ('shadow images') – medical professionals can produce an image of the skeleton and other structures inside the body.
- security checking of baggage – X-rays are used in airports to check the contents of a closed suitcase. Dense structures, such as metals, show up clearly on a monitor.

⮕ **2** State two uses of X-rays.

Bump up your grade

X-ray images are produced by exposing photographic film to X-rays. When an X-ray strikes the film, the film becomes exposed and turns black. Dense structures in the body, such as bone, absorb X-rays – this leaves a 'shadow' region behind the bone which contains no X-rays. Therefore, the film shows where X-rays were and were not absorbed – an image of the bones inside the body.

An X-ray image of a broken leg

F.4g

Uses of gamma rays

Gamma rays are the waves in the electromagnetic spectrum of the highest frequency and highest energy. They are also highly penetrating – several centimetres of lead, or several metres of concrete, are required to absorb gamma rays.

Because of these properties, gamma rays are used for:

- sterilising foods – fresh foods can be exposed to gamma rays, which kill insects, bacteria and moulds that may be present on the foods. This process is known as sterilisation, or **irradiation**. In the UK, tight controls exist around the use of irradiated foods – currently, only dried herbs and spices are allowed to be sterilised in this way. Many consumers are concerned about the potential health effects of eating foods that have been exposed to ionising radiation.
- sterilising medical equipment – gamma rays can kill living tissue, such as bacteria and viruses. Because gamma rays are so penetrating, they can pass straight through thin plastics and metals. Medical equipment can therefore be sterilised using gamma rays. As the waves pass through the equipment, any bacteria or other living organisms are killed. As long as the equipment remains in sealed packaging, it will remain sterile until it is ready to be used.

1 *Name one substance or object that can be sterilised using gamma rays.*

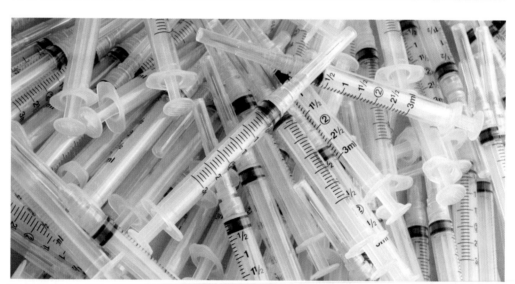

Syringes are often treated with gamma rays, to ensure they are sterile before being used for an injection

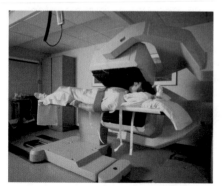

A gamma camera can be used to detect the position of a radioactive tracer in the human body. This can allow doctors to diagnose the type and position of a cancerous tumour.

- detecting cancers – patients who are suspected of having a cancer can be diagnosed using a **radioactive tracer**. This is a small amount of gamma radiation, which is swallowed or injected into the patient. The tracer travels around the body in the bloodstream. It will collect in areas of the body where the cells are most active – like a cancerous tumour. The gamma radiation, because it is so penetrating, can escape from the body and be detected by a **gamma camera**.
- treating cancers – when exposed to gamma radiation, cancerous cells are killed more readily than healthy cells. Gamma radiation can penetrate through the human body. Therefore, gamma radiation can be used to treat a cancerous tumour, even deep inside the body, without the need to operate on a patient.

2 *Why is gamma radiation used to treat cancer cells?*

F.5ab

Some governments advise that children should limit the time spent on a mobile phone, due to the unknown long-term health effects

Dangers of electromagnetic radiation – microwaves and infrared

Microwaves

Over the past few years, **microwaves** have become used very widely for communications, due to:

- their relatively high frequency, which allows microwaves to transfer detailed information (when compared to radio waves)
- their ability to move through the atmosphere without being absorbed.

For example, microwaves are emitted and received by mobile phones, which carry data to and from the phone. Wireless systems, such as Wi-Fi networks, also use microwaves to transfer data from one place to another.

Microwaves are absorbed by water molecules – the energy in the wave is transferred to the water molecule, causing it to heat up. Body cells contain water, therefore, microwaves cause a heating effect in living tissue.

Many people are concerned about the potential health risks associated with long-term exposure to microwave radiation. A number of European governments recommend that steps should be taken to minimise exposure to this type of radiation, for example, by limiting the time a child uses a mobile phone. However, no evidence has been found to date linking a raised level of exposure to microwaves with an increased risk of medical conditions.

⟫ **1** *Why are microwaves used for communications?*

Infrared

Excessive exposure to **infrared** radiation can cause the skin to burn. This permanently damages cells in the skin and can often only be repaired through receiving a skin graft.

Some jobs can cause employees to be exposed to extreme temperatures, for example, welders, metalworkers and firefighters. Exposure to explosive blasts can also cause the same types of injury.

Workers in these professions need to take steps to minimise their exposure to this type of radiation. Steelworkers wear silver coloured suits to reflect the infrared radiation away from their bodies. Reflective goggles perform a similar job, providing protection to the eyes.

⟫ **2** *Which type of injury can exposure to infrared radiation cause?*

Metalworkers can be exposed to high levels of infrared radiation in the workplace

Key words: microwaves, infrared

Bump up your grade

When thinking about the potentially harmful effects of a form of electromagnetic radiation, consider its properties. For example, microwaves cause water molecules to heat up. Body cells contain water. It follows that if a person is exposed to an excessive amount of microwaves, their body cells could be damaged. It is for this reason that it is important for a microwave oven to be checked regularly. This is to make sure microwaves are not leaking out of it into the surrounding environment.

F.5cd

Key points

- Ultraviolet radiation can damage skin cells, leading to skin cancer and eye conditions.
- X-rays and gamma rays can cause damage or mutations to body cells, leading to a range of cancers.

Dangers of electromagnetic radiation – ultraviolet, X-rays and gamma rays

Ultraviolet

Ultraviolet radiation is energetic enough to damage skin and eye cells. It is for this reason that you should use sun screen in the summer months. A cream with a 'Sun Protection Factor' (SPF) 30 will protect your cells from ultraviolet radiation for 30 times longer than using no cream at all.

Tanning of skin is caused by ultraviolet radiation. Overexposure to ultraviolet radiation leads to sunburn – damage to the outer layer of skin cells. This damage can cause skin cells to **mutate**, leading to the formation of skin cancers.

Excessive exposure of the eye to ultraviolet radiation can lead to a condition known as cataracts – clouding of the lens. If left untreated, this can lead to blindness.

▶ **1** *Name one health problem that ultraviolet radiation can cause.*

X-rays and gamma rays

CT scanners provide a detailed image of the internal structures of the body, but also expose the patient to significant levels of X-ray radiation

X-rays and **gamma rays** are the most energetic waves in the **electromagnetic spectrum**. Gamma rays are more energetic than X-rays. However, significant exposure to either type of radiation can be harmful to health. The greater the exposure to the radiation, the greater the risk to health.

Because they are both energetic and penetrating, X-rays and gamma rays can cause mutation or damage to cells inside the body. This can lead to the formation of a cancer.

Medical practitioners have to weigh up the benefits to the patient of exposure to X-rays or gamma rays against the potential health risks. Medical X-rays are of low energy. The benefits gained from having an X-ray usually far outweigh any potential health risks. However, whole-body CT scans expose the patient to significant levels of X-ray radiation, which could cause damage to the body. Therefore these scans are used far less frequently.

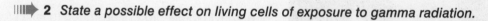

▶ **2** *State a possible effect on living cells of exposure to gamma radiation.*

Exam tip

Gamma radiation can cause cancer. It can also be used to treat cancer. This may seem like a contradiction, but both the harmful effect and the use are linked to the high energy carried by a gamma ray.

Gamma radiation can cause living cells to mutate – this can lead to the formation of a cancer. Gamma radiation can also kill cells – this is how it is used in the treatment of a cancerous tumour.

Key words: mutate, gamma rays, electromagnetic spectrum

1. Which wave in the electromagnetic spectrum has the longest wavelength?

2. Name a wave in the electromagnetic spectrum that travels easily through the Earth's atmosphere.

3. Why is it advisable to wear sun screen when visiting a hot, sunny country?

4. Which form of electromagnetic radiation is emitted by a TV remote control?

5. What is meant by the term 'sterilisation'?

6. What is added to a bank note to help avoid forgery?

7. How is infrared radiation used in burglar alarms?

8. Explain why some people are concerned about living close to a mobile telephone mast.

9. Describe how an X-ray image of a broken bone is produced.

10. Thermal imaging systems have been used to find people trapped under collapsed buildings. Explain how an image would be formed of a survivor.

11. Ultraviolet dyes, which fluoresce when exposed to ultraviolet radiation, are sometimes added to washing powders. Explain how these dyes make whites appear brighter.

Checklist ✓✓✓

Tick when you have:

reviewed it after your lesson ☑ ☐ ☐

revised once – some questions right ☑ ☑ ☐

revised twice – all questions right ☑ ☑ ☑

Move on to another topic when you have all three ticks

Uses of radio waves and microwaves	☐ ☐ ☐
Uses of infrared and visible light	☐ ☐ ☐
Uses of ultraviolet and X-rays	☐ ☐ ☐
Uses of gamma rays	☐ ☐ ☐
Dangers of electromagnetic radiation – microwaves and infrared	☐ ☐ ☐
Dangers of electromagnetic radiation – ultraviolet, X-rays and gamma rays	☐ ☐ ☐

1 **a** What is a wave?

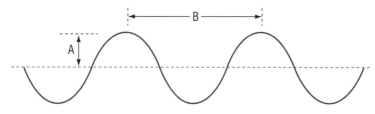

(1 mark)

b On the diagram above, what is represented by:

   i arrow A   *(1 mark)*

   ii arrow B?   *(1 mark)*

c What are the units of wave speed?   *(1 mark)*

d **i** Complete the following sentence:

     Frequency is the number of waves that pass a point ......   *(1 mark)*

   ii What is the frequency of a source that emits 20 waves in 5 seconds? Include the correct unit with your answer.   *(2 marks)*

2 **a** Complete the electromagnetic spectrum below:

	X-rays			Infrared	Microwaves	

(4 marks)

b Which waves:

   i have the highest frequency   *(1 mark)*

   ii have the longest wavelength   *(1 mark)*

   iii carry the most energy?   *(1 mark)*

c Name **one** electromagnetic wave that can cause cancer in humans.   *(1 mark)*

3 Match the wave to its use. Copy the boxes and draw **one** line between each wave and its use.

Microwaves	Detecting forged bank notes
X-rays	Mobile telephone communications
Ultraviolet	TV remote control signals
Infrared	Observing internal structures
Visible light	Sterilising medical equipment
Radio waves	Broadcasting TV signals
Gamma rays	Photography

(7 marks)

Exam tip

Don't forget the units! Quoting the correct units with a numerical answer is often worth a mark in a calculation question. Even if you cannot remember how to do the calculation, writing down a number with the correct unit can often gain you an extra mark.

Exam tip

You will need to be able to recall the order of the electromagnetic spectrum, including the colours of the visible spectrum. The visible colours can be remembered using the mnemonic:

   Longest wavelength, lowest frequency

<u>R</u>ichard	<u>R</u>ed
<u>O</u>f	<u>O</u>range
<u>Y</u>ork	<u>Y</u>ellow
<u>G</u>ave	<u>G</u>reen
<u>B</u>attle	<u>B</u>lue
<u>I</u>n	<u>I</u>ndigo
<u>V</u>ain	<u>V</u>iolet

   Shortest wavelength, highest frequency

4 Infrared radiation can be used for night-vision apparatus. Many police forces have helicopters equipped with night-vision cameras to track suspects in the night time.

   a When does an object emit infrared radiation? *(1 mark)*

   b Complete the following sentence: Infrared radiation has a .... wavelength than visible light. *(1 mark)*

   c Explain why, even in the darkness, a person would be visible on a night-vision camera, even if they could not be seen in the darkness. *(2 marks)*

   d Suggest **one** other application of thermal imaging. *(1 mark)*

5 Gamma rays can be harmful to human health.

   a State **one** harmful effect of excessive exposure to gamma rays. *(1 mark)*

   b State **one** precaution that should be taken when working with gamma rays, to prevent unnecessary exposure. *(1 mark)*

Gamma rays can also be used in ways which are beneficial to human health.

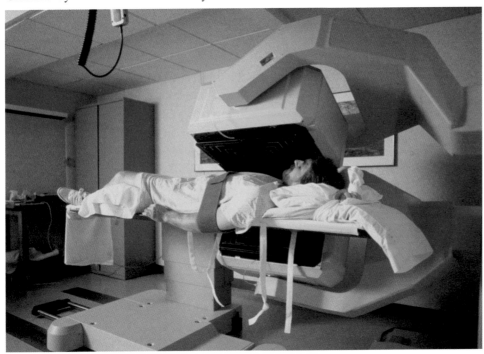

   c By referring to **one** property of gamma radiation, state and explain **one** medical use of gamma radiation. *(4 marks)*

6 **a** **i** What is meant by the **time period** of a wave? *(1 mark)*

      ii How are time period and frequency related? *(1 mark)*

   b Wave speed, frequency and wavelength are related according to the equation:

        wave speed = frequency × wavelength

    What is the wave speed of a **sound** wave of frequency 220 Hz, wavelength 1.5 m? State the appropriate unit for wave speed. *(3 marks)*

   c All electromagnetic waves travel at the speed of light (3×10 m/s) in air.

      i A microwave generator has a frequency of 3 GHz (3.0×10^9 Hz). Calculate the wavelength of the waves, stating an appropriate unit. *(4 marks)*

      ii Long wave radio waves have a wavelength of around 1 km (1000 m). What is the frequency of these waves? State the appropriate unit for frequency. *(4 marks)*

      iii What is the ratio: $\dfrac{\text{frequency of 3 GHz microwaves}}{\text{frequency of 1 km radio waves}}$? *(2 marks)*

How to revise

Prepare

1 Go through the book, completing each section checklist. Only move on to the next section when you have all three ticks for each topic.

2 While doing this, you can decide which are your strong topics, and which are topics that you need to spend more time on.

3 You need to balance your time between:

- **Revising** what you need to know. To do this use the Key points boxes to guide you, and answer the in-text questions and summary questions.
- **Practising** by doing examination-style questions. To do this, answer the examination-style questions at the end of each Learning aim.

Do these two things for each Learning aim in turn.

Revise

4 Think about your best ways of revising. Some of the best ways are to do something *active*. To use active learning you can:

- Write down **notes**, as a summary of the topic. Use highlighter pens to colour key words.
- Make a **poster** to summarise each topic (and perhaps pin it up on your bedroom wall). Make it colourful, and use images/sketches if you can.
- Make a spider-diagram or **mind map** of each topic.
- Ask someone (family or friend) to **test** you on the topic.
- **Teach** the topic to someone (family or friend).

Which method works best for you?

5 It is usually best to work in a quiet room, for about 25–30 minutes at a time, and then take a 5–10 minute break.

6 It is often helpful to draw up a **Revision Calendar**, to keep a note of your progress:

Learning aim A
✓ 3rd April

Practise

7 When you have revised a topic, and think you know it well, then it's important to practise it, by answering some **examination-style questions**.

8 When you have finished them, turn to the **answers** that start on page 114. Can you see how to improve your answers in future?

9 If you have a **Revision Calendar** keep a record of your progress on it.

Learning aim A
✓ 3rd April
✓ 4th April

Re-revise and Top-up

10 It is important to re-revise each topic again, after an interval.
The best intervals are after 10 minutes, after 1 day, and after 1 week.

How to answer questions

Question speak

Command word or phrase	What am I being asked to do?
compare	State the similarities and the differences between two or more things.
complete	Write words or numbers in the gaps provided.
describe	Use words and/or diagrams to say how something looks or how something happens.
describe, as fully as you can	There will be more than one mark for the question so make sure you write the answer in detail.
draw	Make a drawing to show the important features of something.
draw a bar chart / graph	Use given data to draw a bar chart or plot a graph. For a graph, draw a line of best fit.
explain	Apply reasoning to account for the way something is or why something has happened. It is not enough to list reasons without discussing their relevance.
give / name / state	This only needs a short answer without explanation.
list	Write the information asked for in the form of a list.
predict	Say what you think will happen based on your knowledge and using information you may be given.
sketch	A sketch requires less detail than a drawing but should be clear and concise. A sketch graph does not have to be drawn to scale but it should be the appropriate shape and have labelled axes.
suggest	There may be a variety of acceptable answers rather than one single answer. You may need to apply scientific knowledge and/or principles in an unfamiliar context.
use the information	Your answer **must** be based on information given in some form within the question.
what is meant by	You need to give a definition. You may also need to add some relevant comments.

How long should my answer be?

Things to consider:

1 How many lines have been given for the answer?
- One line suggests a single word or sentence. Several lines suggest a longer and more detailed answer is needed.

2 How many marks is the answer worth?
- There is usually one mark for each valid point. So for example, to get all of the marks available for a three mark question you will have to make three different, valid points.

3 As well as lines, is there also a blank space?
- Does the question require you to draw a diagram as part of your answer?
- You may have the option to draw a diagram as part of your answer.

Graphs

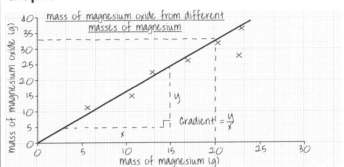

Things to remember:

- Choose sensible scales so the graph takes up most of the grid.
- Don't choose scales that will leave small squares equal to 3 as it is difficult to plot values with sufficient accuracy on such scales.
- Label the axes including units.
- Plot all points accurately by drawing small crosses using a fine pencil.
- Don't try to draw a line through every point. Draw a line of best fit.
- A line of best fit does not have to go through the origin.
- When drawing a line of best fit, don't include any points which obviously don't fit the pattern.
- The graph should have a title stating what it is.
- To find a corresponding value on the y-axis, draw a vertical line from the x-axis to the line on the graph, and a horizontal line across to the y-axis. Find a corresponding value on the x-axis in a similar way.
- The gradient or slope of a line on a graph is the amount it changes on the y-axis divided by the amount it changes on the x-axis. (See the graph above.)

Diagrams

Things to remember:

- Draw diagrams in pencil.
- The diagram needs to be large enough to see any important details.
- Light colouring could be used to improve clarity.
- The diagram should be fully labelled.
- Label lines should be thin and end at the point on the diagram that corresponds to the label.

Calculations

- Write down the equation you are going to use, if it is not already given.
- If you need to, rearrange the equation.
- Make sure that the quantities you put into the equation are in the right units. For example you may need to change centimetres to metres or grams to kilograms.
- Show the stages in your working. Even if your answer is wrong you can still gain method marks.
- If you have used a calculator make sure that your answer makes sense. Try doing the calculation in your head with rounded numbers.
- Give a unit with your final answer, if one is not already given.
- Be neat. Write numbers clearly. If the examiner cannot read what you have written your work will not gain credit. It may help to write a few words to explain what you have done.

Science skills

Science skills are important throughout your course and in your exam.

Make sure that you understand all the words in **bold**.

Collecting evidence (data)

Your evidence needs to be both *repeatable* and *valid*.

Repeatable evidence is data we can trust. If someone else did the same experiment, they would get the same result. It would be **reproducible**.

To make your data more repeatable, repeat your readings and calculate the mean (average).

Valid evidence is data that is repeatable *and* that is relevant to the question being investigated.

Taking measurements

You need to take a **range** of readings that are *accurate* and *precise*.

Accuracy: an expensive thermometer will usually be more accurate than a cheap one. It will give a reading nearer to the *true* temperature.

Precision: a precise instrument will have smaller scale divisions, and will give the same reading again and again under the same conditions. The **spread** of readings will be close together.

Types of variable

- **Categoric** variables: These have word labels, e.g. iron wire, copper wire.
- **Ordered** variables: These are categoric variables that we can put into an order, e.g. small, medium, large.
- **Discrete** variables: These can only have whole number values, e.g. number of layers of insulation keeping a beaker warm, 1, 2, 3.
- **Continuous** variables: These can have any numerical value, e.g. the temperature of water in a beaker, 22.6 °C.

Presenting your data in tables

Independent variable	Dependent variable			
	1st reading	2nd reading	3rd reading	Mean (average)

- **Independent** variable. This is what you change deliberately, step by step. It goes in the first column of the table, and on the horizontal axis of a graph.
- **Dependent** variable. This changes as a result. It goes in the second column(s) of a table, and on the vertical axis of a graph.
- **Control** variables. These should all be kept constant, so that it is a fair test.

Control variables

In field studies and tests on living things, it is difficult to control all the variables, so you need to consider control groups and the size of your samples.

Presenting your data on graphs

A graph shows you what the pattern or relationship is between the two variables.

Choose the best type of graph by looking at the **in**dependent variable.
- If it is a continuous variable – use a line-graph.
- If it is a categoric variable – use a bar chart.

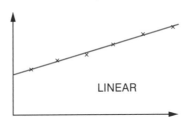

LINEAR

This shows a 'positive linear' relationship. A line sloping down would be 'negative linear'.

The 'line of best fit' gives an average line. Ignore any *anomalous* results.

From the pattern of the graph you should be able to draw a conclusion.

Evaluating an investigation

You need to consider the reproducibility and validity by:
- looking up data from **secondary** sources, e.g. on the internet
- checking the results by using an alternative method
- seeing if other people following the same method get the same results, i.e. are the results reproducible?

Science and society

When making decisions, citizens should look at the evidence, but also ask:
- Is the data **biased**? (e.g. from a company with a commercial interest).
- Is political pressure at work?
- Is the scientist experienced, with a good reputation?

New discoveries often raise difficult issues – these can be ethical, social, economic, or environmental issues.

Tips
- Make sure you are familar with all the **bold** words on these two pages.
- Be clear about the difference between *repeatable* and *valid*, and between *accurate* and *precise*.

Summary

1 Before starting an investigation, it needs to be carefully **planned**, to try to make it a **fair** test.
2 Data (evidence) can be collected by observing and measuring. Results can be recorded in a table and then used to produce a graph.
3 A line of best fit, if appropriate, can help draw a conclusion. From the pattern of the graph you should try to draw a conclusion.
4 Always evaluate an investigation to try to improve it.

Key points

- Units are important – make sure you learn each unit and the abbreviation which should be used.
- You need to learn the equations listed on this page – they will not be provided in the exam.

Formulae you need to learn

Scientific units

Measurement	Unit	Symbol
Power	watts	W
Energy	joules	J
Time	seconds	s
Wave speed	metres per second	m/s
Frequency	hertz	Hz
Wavelength	metres	m

Genetics

There are no specific formulae you need to learn in this section, but remembering these conversions may be helpful when studying genetic crosses:

Probability (chance)	Ratio	Percentage
4 in 4	4 : 0	100%
3 in 4	3 : 1	75%
2 in 4 (simplifies to 1 in 2)	2 : 2 (simplifies to 1 : 1)	50%
1 in 4	1 : 3	25%
0 in 4	0 : 4	0%

Atoms

Number of protons = atomic number

Number of electrons = number of protons

Number of neutrons = mass number − atomic number

$$\text{Relative atomic mass} = \left(\begin{array}{c} \text{proportion} \\ \text{of isotope 1} \end{array} \times \begin{array}{c} A_r \text{ of} \\ \text{isotope 1} \end{array} \right) + \left(\begin{array}{c} \text{proportion} \\ \text{of isotope 2} \end{array} \times \begin{array}{c} A_r \text{ of} \\ \text{isotope 2} \end{array} \right)$$

Formulae you need to know how to use

Electrical energy

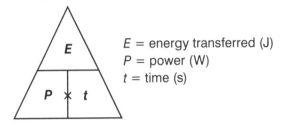

E = energy transferred (J)
P = power (W)
t = time (s)

$$\text{Power (W)} = \frac{\text{energy transferred (J)}}{\text{time (s)}}$$

$$\text{Energy transferred (J)} = \text{power (W)} \times \text{time (s)}$$

$$\text{Time (s)} = \frac{\text{energy transferred (J)}}{\text{power (W)}}$$

$$\text{Cost of electricity} = \text{energy used (units)} \times \text{cost per unit (p)}$$

Efficiency

$$\text{Efficiency (\%)} = \frac{\text{useful energy output}}{\text{total energy input}} \times 100$$

Wave calculations

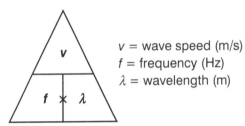

v = wave speed (m/s)
f = frequency (Hz)
λ = wavelength (m)

$$\text{Time period} = \frac{1}{\text{frequency}}$$

$$\text{Wave speed (m/s)} = \text{frequency (Hz)} \times \text{wavelength (m)}$$

$$\text{Wavelength (m)} = \frac{\text{wave speed (m/s)}}{\text{frequency (Hz)}}$$

$$\text{Frequency (Hz)} = \frac{\text{wave speed (m/s)}}{\text{wavelength (m)}}$$

Answers

A Explore cells, organs and genes

A – part 1 (page 9)
1 **Three** from: red blood cell, white blood cell, neurone (motor or sensory), egg cell, sperm cell
2 **One** from: controls the cell, contains genetic information
3 Leaf
4 Groups of organs working together
5 To anchor the plant into the ground, and to absorb water
6 **Two** from: contains digestive enzymes to penetrate the egg, streamlined head, long tail to swim, lots of mitochondria to provide energy for swimming
7 Nucleus, cytoplasm and cell membrane
8 A motor neurone transmits impulses from the CNS to an effector (muscle or gland), whereas a sensory neurone transmits impulses from receptor cells to the CNS
9 Groups of cells work together to form tissues, groups of tissues work together to form organs, groups of organs work together to form organ systems, organ systems work together to form organisms
10 Xylem vessels are made of dead cells, joined together with no end walls, whereas phloem vessels are made of living cells with small holes in the end cell walls, which allow substances to pass through
11 As water evaporates from the leaves through the stomata, more water is pulled up through the xylem to replace it. This causes water to be drawn in from the roots to replace the water that is lost, providing a continuous stream of water.

A – part 2 (page 21)
1 In the nucleus of cells
2 A dominant allele will always be expressed if it is present in the nucleus
3 A section of DNA, gene, chromosome, nucleus, cell
4 The DNA sequence of an organism is changed
5 A heterozygous organism contains two different alleles for a characteristic, whereas a homozygous organism contains two of the same alleles for a characteristic
6 TAAGCATGTC
7 a Freckles
  b No freckles
  c Freckles
8 a A carrier of cystic fibrosis will be healthy, however they will have one copy of the disorder-causing allele
  b 3 healthy children : 1 cystic fibrosis sufferer
9 a

	D	d
D	DD	Dd
d	Dd	dd

  b 75% of children born will be sufferers
  c Both are sufferers

Answers to Examination-style questions

Learning aim A (pages 22–23)
1 a i Cytoplasm (1)
   ii Respiration (1)
   iii Controls the cell (1) Contains the genetic material/instructions to make a new cell (1)
  b i Animals do not carry out photosynthesis (1)
   ii Cell wall (1) Vacuole (1)
2 a i Cells have special features, which enable them to perform their function (1)
   ii A Nerve/neurone (1) B Sperm (1) C Root hair (1) D White blood cell (1)
  b i To transport oxygen around the body (1)
   ii No nucleus and flattened disc (1) to maximise the surface area for carrying oxygen (1)
3 a i Transpiration stream (1)
   ii Root hair cell (1)
   iii Large hair (1) and large vacuole (1) increase the surface area allowing more water to be absorbed (1)
  b i As water evaporates (1) from the air spaces in leaves, more water is pulled up through the xylem to take its place (1)
   ii Increased temperature (1) – increased rate of evaporation (1);
Decreased humidity (1) – increased rate of evaporation (1);
Increased wind strength (1) – increased rate of evaporation (1)
[Max. 2 – 1 mark for factor and 1 mark for an appropriate explanation]
4 a i

Structure	Cell	Organ
Kidney		✓	(1)
Sperm	✓		(1)
Liver		✓	(1)

   ii A group of cells working together to perform a function (1)
  b A group of cells (1), such as muscle cells (1), work together to form tissues (1), such as muscle (1). Tissues work together to form organs (1) such as the heart (1). Organs, such as the heart and lungs work together to form organ systems (1), such as the circulatory system (1). Organ systems work together to form an organism (1).
[Max. 6 – 1 mark for explanation of a level of organisation and 1 mark for appropriate example]
5 a i (Male) with attached ear lobes (1)
   ii (Female) with unattached ear lobes (1)
  b i Recessive (1) Two parents with unattached earlobes are able to have offspring with attached earlobes (1), therefore they must be heterozygous/carry a recessive allele for attached ear lobes (1)
   ii ee (1) [Answer requires two identical lowercase letters]
   iii Ee (1) [Answer requires one uppercase and one lowercase letter, of the same letter]
They must be heterozygous/carrier of the recessive allele (1) to be able to pass the recessive allele/allele coding for attached ear lobes to their child (1)

6 a i A carrier has one copy of the recessive allele (1) but does not have the disease (1)
   ii Tt (1)
  b i Tt x Tt (1) offspring: TT, Tt, Tt, tt (1)
or

	T	t
T	TT	Tt
t	Tt	tt

(2)

   ii 1 in 4 (1)
   iii 50% (1)

B Explore the roles of the nervous and endocrine systems in homeostasis and communication

B – part 1 (page 30)
1 To transmit chemical messages around the body
2 The CNS consists of the brain and the spinal cord. The PNS consists of motor neurones and sensory neurones.
3 Voluntary responses require thought, involuntary responses occur without thinking
4 **Two** from: internal temperature, blood glucose (sugar levels), body water concentration, carbon dioxide levels, oxygen levels, etc.
5 a Reflex
  b Voluntary
  c Voluntary
  d Reflex
6 When the impulse reaches the end of the axon, chemicals are released. These diffuse across the synapse and bind to receptors on the next neurone. This triggers an impulse in the next neurone.
7 It has a long axon, to transmit impulses over long distances. The axon is covered in a fatty sheath to speed up the impulse and prevent it being scrambled. They have branched endings at either end of the cell, allowing the neurone to connect with many other neurones.
8 Reflex actions are quicker as they do not involve the brain, meaning the nerve pathway is shorter, resulting in the reaction being faster. Speed is essential as the reactions are often used to get an organism out of danger.
9 Stimulus – being stung → detected by pain receptor in the toe → sensory neurone → spinal cord → motor neurone → effector – muscles in the leg contract → response – move the toe away from the bee

B – part 2 (page 35)
1 They travel in the blood
2 Glucose is used in respiration to release energy
3 A store of glucose
4 Blood capillaries dilate (vasodilation), hairs lower/lie flat and person sweats
5 As the water in sweat evaporates, heat energy is lost from the skin, cooling the body
6 Vasodilation is when the vessels supplying capillaries in the skin dilate, increasing blood flow to the surface of the skin. Vasoconstriction is when the vessels supplying capillaries in the skin constrict, decreasing blood flow to the surface of the skin.
7 Nervous response – very fast, as transmitted via electrical impulses; are short acting; cause an effect in a very precise area. Hormonal response

– slower response, as hormones travel in the blood; are longer acting; cause an effect over a larger area.

8 a The brain contains receptors that monitor the blood's temperature. Temperature receptors in the skin also send information to the brain about the skin's temperature. When a change in body temperature is detected, the brain causes different parts of the body to respond, to return the body temperature to normal.

b High temperatures can result in dehydration/fits. Low temperature results in slowed movement/can induce a coma.

9 a If the blood glucose concentration is too high, insulin is released. Insulin makes the liver remove glucose from the blood, by turning glucose into glycogen. As there is now less glucose in the blood, blood glucose concentration falls.

b If the blood glucose concentration is too low, the pancreas releases glucagon. Glucagon makes the liver change glycogen back into glucose. This is then released into the blood, causing blood glucose concentration to rise.

Answers to Examination-style questions

➤➤ **Learning aim B (pages 36–37)**

1 a i Stand up/are erect (1)
   ii Do not release sweat (1)
   iii Constrict/narrow (1)
  b Shivering (1) more energy is needed for muscles to contract (1) heat released from respiration (1)

2 a

	Nerves	Hormones
Speed of communication	Very fast	**Slow(er)**
Method of transport/ transmission	**Electrical impulse**	In the blood
Duration of response	Short	**Long(er)**

(3) [1 mark for each correct answer – shown in bold type]

  b chemical (1) glands (1) target organs (1)
  c Any hormone named, e.g. testosterone, glucagon, insulin, oestrogen (1)

3 a Homeostasis (1)
  b Nervous system (1) and endocrine/hormonal system (1)
  c For example, **one** from:
   Internal temperature (1) to allow enzymes to work optimally (1)
   Oxygen levels (1) to allow respiration to occur (1)
   Carbon dioxide (1) to prevent build-up of toxic waste (1)

4 a Faster response (1)
  b

Activity	Voluntary response	Involuntary response
Pupils in your eyes contract in bright light		✓
Kick a ball	✓	
Sign your name	✓	
Removing your hand from a hot saucepan		✓

(2) [4 ticks correct, 2 marks; 2 or 3 ticks correct, 1 mark]

  c i Motor neurone (1)
   ii Relay neurone/neurone B (1)
   iii Muscle/biceps (1)
  d Impulse would travel to the brain (1)

5 a i To release energy during respiration (1)
   ii After the person has eaten (1)
   iii Food has been digested releasing glucose into the bloodstream (1) raising blood glucose concentration (1)
  b i Insulin (1)
   ii Insulin makes the liver remove glucose from the blood (1) by turning glucose into glycogen (1). As there is now less glucose in the blood, blood glucose concentration falls. (1)
  c i Glucagon (1)
   ii Glucagon makes the liver (1) change glycogen back into glucose (1). This is then released into the blood, causing blood glucose concentration to rise. (1)

6 a 37 °C (1) [Unit must be stated to award the mark]
  b i Thermoregulatory centre (1)
   ii Receptors in the brain monitor the blood's temperature. (1) Temperature receptors in the skin send information to the brain about the skin's temperature. (1) The brain processes this information and coordinates a response. (1)
  c Vasodilation is when the vessels supplying capillaries in the skin dilate (1), increasing blood flow to the surface of the skin (1) and heat is lost by radiation (1).
   Vasoconstriction is when the vessels supplying capillaries in the skin constrict (1), decreasing blood flow to the surface of the skin (1), reducing heat loss by radiation (1).

C Explore atomic structure and the periodic table

➤➤ **C – part 1 (page 44)**

1 Diagram should have a central labelled nucleus, with electrons orbiting around the nucleus
2 **Three** from: strong; can be hammered into shape; good conductors of heat; good conductors of electricity
3 a C
  b H
  c O

4

Particle	Relative charge	Relative mass
Proton	Positive	1
Neutron	Neutral	1
Electron	Negative	Almost zero

5 It is located to the left of the 'staircase'
6 Atomic mass is the number of protons, whereas mass number is the number of neutrons and protons
7 19 electrons
8 a Zn
  b 65
  c 30
9 a 15
  b 16
  c Neutral – it contains equal numbers of protons and electrons so the positive and negative charges cancel out

➤➤ **C – part 2 (page 51)**

1 Same group
2 7
3 Closest to

4 Diagrams should contain the following **a** 2 shells: 2 electrons in the first shell, 4 in the second. **b** 3 shells: 2 electrons in the first shell, 8 electrons in the second shell, 2 electrons in the third shell. **c** 3 shells: 2 electrons in the first shell, 8 electrons in the second shell, 4 electrons in the third shell **d** 3 shells: 2 electrons in the first shell, 8 electrons in the second shell, 5 electrons in the third shell.

5 a 2.4
  b 2.8.2
  c 2.8.4
  d 2.8.5

6 They will be different densities and one may be radioactive

7 They have the same chemical properties as they have the same number of electrons. They have different physical properties as they have different numbers of neutrons.

8 The relative atomic mass takes into the account the mass of all naturally occurring isotopes of an element and the frequency with which these occur

9 $(0.08 \times 6) + (0.92 \times 7) = 6.92$

Answers to Examination-style questions

➤➤ **Learning aim C (pages 52–53)**

1 a i Nucleus (1)
   ii Neutrons (1) Protons (1)
  b i 5 (1)
   ii Negative (1)
  c i Aluminium/Gallium/Indium/Thallium (1)
   ii Non-metal (1) it is on the right-hand side of the ('staircase' in) the periodic table (1)

2 a one (1) centre/middle (1) shells/energy levels (1) closest/nearest (1)
  b

Particle	Relative charge	Relative mass
Proton	+1	1
Neutron	0	1
Electron	−1	(Almost) zero

(3) [1 mark for each correct answer – shown in bold type]

3 a Fe (1)
  b i 26 (1)
   ii 26 (1)
   iii (Neutrons = mass number − atomic number) 56 − 26 = 30 (1)
  c Neutral/zero (1) It contains equal numbers of protons and electrons, so the positive and negative charges are equal (1)

4 a 14 (1)
  b i 7 (1)
   ii 2 electrons in the first shell (1), 5 electrons in the second shell (1)
  c i It has the same chemical properties as nitrogen/has the same number of electrons in its outer shell (1)
   ii Group 5 (1)
   iii Group number is same as number of electrons in atom's outer shell (1)
  d 2.8.5 [2 marks if 3 shells correct, 1 mark if 2 shells correct]

5 a i Same number of protons/same number of electrons (1)
   ii Different number of neutrons (1)
  b i Isotopes (of copper) (1)

ii [Max. of 4 marks] They will have the same chemical properties (1) as they have the same number of electrons in the outer shell (1), therefore will react in the same way (1). They will have different physical properties (1), for example, density (1), as the mass of one atom is greater (1).

c Relative atomic mass takes into account mass of naturally occurring isotopes of an element (1) and relative abundance of these isotopes (1)

6 a i Mg (1)

ii 14 (1)

iii 2.8.2 (2) [2 marks for 3 shells correct, 1 mark for 2 shells correct]

b Relative atomic mass = proportion × relative atomic mass (1) = $(0.79 \times 24) + (0.10 \times 25) + (0.11 \times 26)$ (1) = 24.32 (1)

D Explore substances and chemical reactions

D – part 1 (page 60)

1 Acid – hydrochloric acid, lemon juice; alkali – sodium hydroxide, ammonia

2 a Zinc oxide

b Zinc, oxygen

3 An element contains only one type of atom, whereas a compound contains more than one type of atom chemically bonded together

4 Alkalis are soluble in water, whereas bases are insoluble

5 Mixtures are substances that are 'mixed' together, whereas the substances in a compound are chemically bound together

6 1 copper atom, 1 sulfur atom and 4 oxygen atoms

7 Acids produce positive hydrogen ions when they dissolve in water, whereas alkalis produce negative hydroxide ions when they dissolve in water

8 $2H_2 + O_2 \rightarrow 2H_2O$

9 $4Al + 3O_2 \rightarrow 2Al_2O_3$

D – part 2 (page 69)

1 Universal indicator and litmus paper

2 a 7

b Green

c It will stay blue

3 Put a lighted splint in the gas – it will produce a squeaky pop if it contains hydrogen

4 a Irritant

b Wear eye protection and wash any spills off skin immediately

5 a Magnesium chloride

b Magnesium sulfate

c Magnesium nitrate

6 a Sodium hydrogen carbonate or magnesium hydroxide

b Indigestion is caused by excess acid. Antacids contain weak alkalis. These work by neutralising the excess acid produced by the stomach.

7 a Sulfuric acid + zinc oxide → zinc sulfate + water

b $H_2SO_4 + ZnO \rightarrow ZnSO_4 + H_2O$

8 a Hydrochloric acid + copper carbonate → copper chloride + water + carbon dioxide

b $2HCl + CuCO_3 \rightarrow CuCl_2 + H_2O + CO_2$

Answers to Examination-style questions

Learning aim D (pages 70–71)

1 a

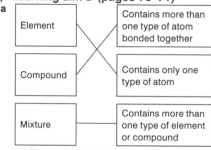

(3) [1 mark for each correct connecting line]

b i Compound (1)

ii One carbon atom (1) and two oxygen atoms (1)

2 a i A (1)

ii C (1)

iii Flammable (1)

b Any **two** from: wear eye protection/goggles (1) wear gloves (1) do not use near naked flame (1) store in secure (flammables) unit (1)

c D (1)

3 a i B (1) It contains two different atoms bonded together (1)

ii D (1) It contains two compounds, which are not joined together (1) *or* E (1) It contains two elements, which are not joined together (1)

iii Molecules of an element (1)

b i A (1) It is an element/all the atoms are the same (1)

ii C (1) Nitrogen exists as molecules made up of two identical atoms bonded together/diatomic molecules (1)

c 2 atoms of iron (1) bonded to 3 atoms of oxygen (1)

4 a i Hydrochloric acid (1)

ii Red (1)

iii Sodium carbonate (1)

b Water (1)

c Bubble through lime water (1) Lime water turns from clear to cloudy if carbon dioxide is present (1)

5 a i Acid + metal (1 mark for reactants) → salt + hydrogen (1 mark for products)

ii Put a lit splint into a test tube; it will go pop if hydrogen is present (1)

b Aluminium sulfate (1)

c $2HCl + Zn \rightarrow ZnCl_2 + H_2$ (1 mark for reactants, 1 mark for products, 1 mark for balanced equation)

d Group 1 metals are extremely reactive (1) The reaction would result in an explosion (1)

6 a i Acidic lake water will turn yellow/orange/pink/red with universal indicator (1) Once neutralised it will turn green with universal indicator (1)

ii pH 7 (1)

iii An alkali is a base that will dissolve in water (1)

b i Hydrochloric acid + calcium carbonate (1 mark for reactants) → calcium chloride (1 mark for correct salt) + carbon dioxide + water (1 mark for correct other products)

ii $2HCl + CaCO_3$ (1 mark for reactants) → $CaCl_2 + CO_2 + H_2O$ (1 mark for products and 1 mark for balanced equation)

c Lime is added to acidic soil (1), because most plants prefer to grow in a neutral soil (1)

E Explore the importance of energy stores, energy transfers and energy transformations

E – part 1 (page 78)

1 Thermal, electrical, light, sound, mechanical and nuclear energy

2 Chemical, kinetic, gravitational potential, elastic potential, thermal and nuclear energy

3 Mechanically, electrically, by conduction, by convection and by radiation

4 Energy stored in an object that is in a raised position relative to another object

5 Elastic potential energy

6 Mechanical energy can be kinetic energy, or one of the forms of potential energy – gravitational potential or elastic potential

7 By conduction, convection or thermal radiation

8 Convection currents require the particles of the medium to be able to move. In a solid, the particles are fixed in position and so cannot allow convection currents to form.

9 A chemical reaction occurs, which results in the formation of chemical bonds. This releases energy, often in the form of thermal energy.

10 Nuclear fuels have a very high energy density – they release a large quantity of energy from a small mass of fuel

11 Part of a fluid is heated → this causes this section of the fluid to expand → this makes this part of the fluid less dense → this causes the warmed section of the fluid to rise. The reverse process occurs to the cooler parts of the fluid.

E – part 2 (page 89)

1 Energy cannot be created or destroyed, only **transferred from one form to another**

2 Any **five** from: solar, wind, biofuels, hydroelectric, wave, tidal, geothermal

3 Watts (W) or joules per second (J/s)

4 Nuclear fuel (uranium or plutonium)

5 $Power = \dfrac{energy}{time}$

6 A battery carries out a chemical reaction, resulting in a transfer of chemical → electrical energy. A fuel cell produces the same energy transfer, but requires a constant supply of fuel to operate.

7 Because they do not operate 24 hours per day, 365 days per year. Solar cells do not work at night time and wind turbines do not operate when there is no wind or when the wind speed is dangerously high.

8 $Power = \dfrac{energy}{time} = \dfrac{4500}{5} = 900\,W$

9 Any device with moving parts experiences friction – this produces wasted thermal energy. Any device which is electrical produces thermal energy as the electric current flows through wires.

10 Nuclear fission → release of thermal energy → heats water to steam → steam turns turbines → turbines turn generators → generators convert kinetic energy into electrical energy

11 Useful energy output = efficiency × total energy input = $0.25 \times 200 = 50\,J$
Wasted energy = total energy input − useful energy output = $200 - 50 = 150\,J$

Answers to Examination-style questions

Learning aim E (pages 90–91)

1 a Kinetic (1), Nuclear (1)
  b i Electrical energy (1)
    ii Light energy (1), Sound energy (1)
    iii Thermal energy (1)
2 a i Useful energy is the energy transferred by a device which is wanted (1)
    ii Wasted energy is the energy transferred by a device which is not wanted (1)
  b Electrical energy (1) → light energy (1) + thermal energy (1)   ↑
          ↑   useful (1)
       wasted (1)
  c Wasted energy is lost to the atmosphere (1)
3 a i Renewable – the energy source will never run out if replenished (1)
    ii Non-renewable – the energy source will run out in the future (1)
  b

Energy source	Renewable?	Non-renewable?
Coal		✓
Solar	✓	
Geothermal	✓	
Nuclear		✓
Wind	✓	

(5) [4 correct, 2 marks; 3 or 2 correct, 1 mark; 1 or 0 correct, 0 marks]

4

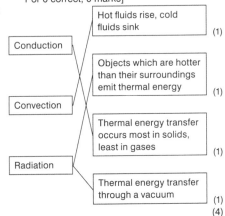

Conduction — Hot fluids rise, cold fluids sink (1)
Convection — Objects which are hotter than their surroundings emit thermal energy (1)
Radiation — Thermal energy transfer occurs most in solids, least in gases (1)
— Thermal energy transfer through a vacuum (1)
(4)

5 a Liquid or gas (1)
  b Hot fluids rise, cold fluids sink (1)
  c i Arrow downwards on cold air side plus arrow upwards on hot air side (1), arrow pointing left anywhere inside the chimney (1)
    ii The hot air expands (1) and becomes less dense (1). This means it rises. (1) [Accept reverse argument]
6 a 4500 J (1)
  b $\frac{1500}{6000} \times 100$ (1) = 25% (1)
  c $\frac{6000}{6}$ (1) = 1000 (1) [Accept 1 if unit is kW] W or J/s (1)
7 a Cost = 12 × 15 (1) = 180 = £1.80 (1)
  b LED uses $\frac{1}{3}$ energy of 'energy-saving' (1)
     = $\frac{180}{3}$ (1) = 60p = £0.60 (1)

c [Marking points – max. 6]:
  • LED bulb has higher initial cost/'energy-saving' has lower initial cost (1)
  • LED bulb is cheaper to run/uses less energy/'energy-saving' is more expensive to run/uses more energy (1)
  • LED bulb more efficient/'energy-saving' less efficient (1)
  • Calculation: LED bulb 75% efficient/'energy-saving' 25% efficient (1)
  • Calculation: 'energy-saving' bulb costs 3 times as much to run (1)
  • LED bulb will last for longer/'energy-saving' will need replacing more quickly (1)
  • Calculation: LED bulb will last 25 times longer (1)
  • In the long term, LED bulb will be the cheaper option (1)
  • After 16 000 hours, 'energy-saving' bulb replacement cost is greater than LED bulb replacement cost (1)
  • Calculation: over the lifetime of the LED bulb, 'energy-saving' bulb replacement cost is more than three times the replacement cost of LED bulb (1)
  • LED bulb contributes less to global warming through lower energy consumption (1)

F Explore the properties and applications of waves in the electromagnetic spectrum

F – part 1 (page 98)

1 Statement b is correct – All waves are energy carriers
2 The speed of light (3×10^8 m/s)
3 Seven
4 Wave speed = frequency × wavelength
5 Gamma rays (highest frequency), X-rays, ultraviolet, visible light, infrared, microwaves, radio waves (lowest frequency)
6 Longitudinal – the wave vibrations are parallel to the direction of wave motion. Transverse – the wave vibrations are perpendicular to the direction of wave motion.
7 Any **three** from: radio waves, microwaves, infrared, visible light, ultraviolet, X-rays, gamma rays
8 a i Amplitude – the mean position to a peak, or trough, of the wave
    ii Wavelength – the peak-to-peak, or trough-to-trough, distance
  b P will move up and down, as the wave passes left to right
9 a 1×10^2
  b 3×10^5
  c 2.55×10^6
  d 3×10^{-4}
  e 6.7×10^{-6}
10 a Frequency = $\frac{400}{20}$ = 20 Hz
   b Time period = $\frac{1}{20}$ = 0.05 s
   c Wavelength = $\frac{\text{wave speed}}{\text{frequency}}$ = $\frac{340}{20}$ = 17 m

F – part 2 (page 105)

1 Radio waves
2 Choice from: radio waves, microwaves, infrared, visible light
3 Sunlight contains ultraviolet radiation, which can damage skin cells. Sun cream absorbs ultraviolet radiation, therefore protecting your skin.
4 Infrared
5 Sterilisation means killing all living organisms – including bacteria, viruses and other microorganisms
6 Ultraviolet ink
7 An infrared beam is made between an emitter and the detector. This is invisible to the naked eye. If an intruder breaks the beam, the alarm will go off.
8 Excessive exposure to microwave radiation has been linked with the heating of internal body cells. Some people are concerned that this poses a risk to human health.
9 Patient stands in front of photographic film → patient is exposed to X-rays → when X-rays strike bone, they are absorbed → bone produces a shadow region, leaving this part of the film unexposed → when X-rays meet soft tissue, they pass straight through, reaching the film → the X-rays that reach the film turn the film black → a crack or break in a bone would allow X-rays through to the film, and so shows up as a black line or region against a white (bone) background
10 The survivor would be hotter than their surroundings (parts of the collapsed building) and so would emit thermal radiation. This is detected by the imaging system and converted into an image for the operator.
11 When a washed garment is exposed to sunlight, ultraviolet radiation would strike the clothing. This would cause the dye to fluoresce (give out light) and make the clothing appear brighter (and therefore cleaner).

Answers to Examination-style questions

Learning aim F (pages 106–107)

1 a A wave is an energy carrier (1)
  b i Arrow A = amplitude (1)
    ii Arrow B = wavelength (1)
  c Metres per second (m/s) (1)
  d i Frequency is the number of waves that pass a point **per second** (1)
    ii 4 (1) Hz (1)
2 a (4) [1 mark for each correct answer – shown in bold type]

Gamma rays
X-rays
Ultraviolet
Visible light
Infrared
Microwaves
Radio waves

  b i Gamma rays (1)
    ii Radio waves (1)
    iii Gamma rays (1)
  c **One** from: gamma rays/X-rays/ultraviolet (1)

3

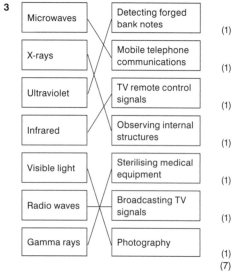

Microwaves	Detecting forged bank notes (1)
X-rays	Mobile telephone communications (1)
Ultraviolet	TV remote control signals (1)
Infrared	Observing internal structures (1)
Visible light	Sterilising medical equipment (1)
Radio waves	Broadcasting TV signals (1)
Gamma rays	Photography (1)
	(7)

4 a When the object is hotter than its surroundings (1)

b Infrared radiation has a **longer** wavelength than visible light (1)

c The person would emit infrared radiation (1), which would be detected/displayed by the camera (1)

d Any **one** from: military use, e.g. for seeing the enemy at night time/locating survivors in collapsed buildings/monitoring heat loss, e.g. from a building/medical uses, e.g. screening for breast cancer/alternative correct response (1)

5 a One from: damage or mutation of cells/ cancer (1)

b One from: keep distance from source of radiation/protective clothing/(lead) shielding/ minimise exposure time (1)

c One from:
Use: Medical imaging (1)
Property: Penetration (1)
Explanation (two from): Tracer is inserted into patient. (1) Tracer collects at target organ. (1) Gamma radiation emitted (1) which is detected by a gamma camera (1).
Use: (Internal) radiotherapy (1)
Property: Gamma radiation kills cells (1)
Explanation (two from): Gamma source inserted into patient. (1) Gamma radiation incident on tumour. (1) Cancer cells are killed by gamma radiation. (1)

Use: (External) radiotherapy (1)
Property: Penetration/gamma radiation kills cells (1)
Explanation (two from): Patient is exposed to gamma rays from outside the body. (1) Gamma radiation penetrates inside the body to the tumour. (1) Cancer cells are killed by gamma radiation. (1)

6 a i Time taken to produce one wave/time for one complete wave to pass a point (1)

ii Time period $= \dfrac{1}{\text{frequency}}$ (1)

b Wave speed $= 220 \times 1.5$ (1) $= \mathbf{330}$ (1) **m/s** (1)

c i Wavelength $= \dfrac{\text{wave speed}}{\text{frequency}}$ (1) $= \dfrac{3 \times 10^8}{3 \times 10^9}$

(1) $= \mathbf{0.1}$ (1) **m** (1)

ii Frequency $= \dfrac{\text{wave speed}}{\text{wavelength}}$ (1) $= \dfrac{3 \times 10^8}{1000}$

(1) $= \mathbf{3 \times 10^5}$ (1) **Hz** (1)

iii Ratio $= \dfrac{3 \times 10^9}{3 \times 10^5}$ (1) $= \mathbf{10\,000 : 1}$ (2)

Glossary

A

acid: Chemical with a pH of less than 7.

adenine: A DNA base, which forms complementary bonds with thymine.

alkali: Base which is soluble in water.

allele: A version of a specific gene.

amplitude: The height of a wave – measured from the mean position to a peak, or to a trough.

antacid: A drug containing a weak alkali, which is used to treat indigestion.

antibodies: Chemicals which 'deactivate' microorganisms preventing them causing disease.

atom: The smallest part of an element that can still be recognised as that element.

atomic nucleus: The very small, central part of an atom that contains protons and neutrons.

atomic number: The number of protons in an atom (sometimes called the proton number).

B

balanced equation: A chemical reaction that has the same mass of reactants and products.

base: Chemical with a pH of greater than 7.

battery: A device that converts chemical energy to electrical energy. Contains the required reactants for the energy transfer.

biofuel: Fuel made from animal or plant products.

C

carbon neutral: A process that uses as much carbon dioxide as it produces.

carbonate: A chemical which reacts with an acid to produce a salt, carbon dioxide and water.

carrier: A person who has a heterozygous genotype, containing one copy of a healthy dominant allele and one copy of a disorder causing recessive allele. A carrier shows no symptoms of the disorder.

cell membrane: Structure surrounding a cell, which controls what can come in and out of a cell.

cell wall: A rigid structure that surrounds plant cells.

cells: The building blocks of all living organisms.

central nervous system (CNS): This is made up of the brain and the spinal cord and is where information is processed.

chemical bond: An attractive force which is formed between atoms when a molecule is produced.

chemical energy: Energy contained in an object due to the chemical reactions within it.

chemical equation: A description of the reactants and products in a chemical reaction.

chemical formula: This shows the chemical 'make up' of a substance – it tells you the type and number of each atom present.

chemical symbol: An international code used to represent each element in the periodic table.

chloroplast: The component in a plant cell in which photosynthesis takes place.

chromosome: Length of DNA carrying a number of genes.

clones: Offspring produced by asexual reproduction, which are genetically identical to their parent.

compound: A substance made from two or more elements chemically bonded together.

conduction: Transfer of thermal energy from particle to particle.

conductor: Material that transmits thermal energy.

convection current: Thermal energy transfer through a fluid by the movement of particles.

cytoplasm: Jelly-like substance present in a cell where chemical reactions take place.

cytosine: A DNA base which forms complementary bonds with guanine.

D

dense: Mass of an object divided by volume – the mass per unit volume of an object.

dissipate: To give out into the atmosphere, in a dilute form.

DNA: Deoxyribonucleic acid – the material of inheritance.

dominant allele: The characteristics that these alleles code for will always be expressed if a dominant allele is present in the nucleus.

E

effectors: Muscles and glands that respond to nervous impulses.

efficiency: Amount of useful energy transferred by a device, divided by the total energy supplied to a device.

elastic potential energy: Energy stored in an object which has been stretched.

electromagnetic (e.m.) spectrum: A family of waves that have different frequencies and wavelengths, but all travel at a very high speed.

electron shells: The organisation of electrons into energy levels.

electronic configuration: A set of numbers to show the arrangement of electrons into shells (or energy levels).

electron: A subatomic particle, with a relative negative charge, that orbits the nucleus of an atom.

element: A substance made up of only one type of atom.

energy source: This is used to produce electrical energy from a range of different origins.

energy store: A supply of energy, which can be saved to use at a later time.

engulf: The process by which a white blood cell destroys a microorganism by 'swallowing' it.

F

flammable: Chemical which is able to combust.

fluid: A liquid or a gas.

fluorescent: An object that gives out light, after stimulation by an energy source.

fossil fuels: Fuels obtained from fossilised plant and animal material – coal, oil or natural gas.

frequency: The number of waves passing a fixed point every second.

fuel cell: A device that converts chemical energy to electrical energy. Requires continual supply of reactants for the energy transfer.

G

gamma camera: A detector that converts gamma rays into a visible image.

gamma rays: High-energy electromagnetic radiation.

gene: A short section of DNA that contains the genetic information to code for a characteristic.

genetic diagram: A diagram that shows the potential offspring from a genetic cross.

genetically inherited disorder: A disease that can be passed on to offspring through their genetic material.

genotype: The alleles an organism has for a specific characteristic.

glands: Organs that produce fluids such as hormones and sweat.

glucagon: A hormone involved in the control of blood glucose concentration.

glycogen: Store of carbohydrates.

gravitational potential energy: Energy an object contains due to its position in a gravitational field.

group: All the elements in one column of the periodic table. The group number tells you the number of electrons an atom has in its outer shell.

guanine: A DNA base that forms complementary bonds with cytosine.

H

haemoglobin: The red pigment found in blood cells, which binds to oxygen molecules.

hazard symbol: A symbol that indicates the potential danger of using a chemical.

heterozygous: Describes an organism that contains two different alleles for a characteristic.

homeostasis: The maintenance of constant internal body conditions.

homozygous: Describes an organism that contains two identical alleles for a characteristic.

hormones: Chemical messengers that transport information around the body.

I

indicator: Chemicals that change colour in the presence of an acid or an alkali.

infrared: Electromagnetic waves between visible light and microwaves in the electromagnetic spectrum.

insulator: A material that does not allow thermal energy to pass through it easily.

insulin: A hormone involved in the control of blood glucose concentration.

inversely proportional: Two related factors – as one increases, the other decreases.

involuntary response: An automatic rapid response that occurs without thinking. Also known as a reflex.

irradiation: The exposure of an object or material to ionising radiation.

isotopes: Forms of an element with the same number of protons, but different numbers of neutrons.

J

joule: The unit of energy.

K

kilowatt-hour: The electrical energy supplied to a 1 kW electrical device in one hour.

kinetic energy: Energy of a moving object.

L

law of conservation of energy: Energy cannot be created or destroyed, only transferred from one form to another.

leaf: Plant organ whose primary function is to photosynthesise to produce glucose.

liming: Adding lime or powdered limestone to neutralise a soil or a lake.

litmus paper: An indicator used to test if a solution is acidic or alkaline.

longitudinal: A type of wave, where the vibrations are parallel to the direction of wave motion.

luminous: An object that emits light.

M

mass number: The total number of neutrons and protons in an atom. Also known as atomic mass.

mesophyll: Plant tissue that carries out photosynthesis.

metal: Elements that are strong, can be hammered into shape and are good conductors of heat and electricity.

microwaves: A form of electromagnetic radiation.

mitochondria: The component of a cell in which respiration takes place.

mixture: A substance made up of different elements and/or compounds that are not chemically bonded together.

molecule: Two or more atoms, chemically bonded together.

monohybrid inheritance: Study of the inheritance of one characteristic coded for by a single gene.

motor neurone: A neurone that carries impulses from the CNS to an effector.

mutate: Change an organism's DNA.

mutation: A change in an organism's genetic material.

N

National Grid: The network of cables and transformers used to transfer electricity around the country.

nerves: A tissue consisting of bundles of hundreds or even thousands of axons.

neutral: Chemical with a pH of 7.

neutralisation: Chemical reaction of an acid and base, which results in a neutral solution being made.

neutron: A subatomic particle found in the nucleus of an atom. It has no electrical charge.

newton: The unit of force.

non-metal: All elements which are not metals. They are poor conductors of heat and electricity.

non-renewable: An energy source that cannot be replaced once it has been used up.

nuclear decay: The process of an unstable nucleus emitting ionising radiation.

nuclear fission: The process in which certain nuclei split into two fragments, releasing energy.

nucleus (of an atom): *see atomic nucleus.*

nucleus (of a cell): Component of a plant and animal cell that contains the genetical material and controls what the cell does.

O

optical fibre: Thin glass fibre, through which light and infrared signals can be sent.

organ: A group of different tissues working together to perform a particular function.

organ system: A group of organs working together to perform a particular function.

organism: A group of organ systems working together to form a fully functional plant or animal.

oscillate: Vibrate about a point.

oscillations: Vibrations about a fixed point.

oxidation: A chemical reaction where oxygen is added to a substance.

P

pathogens: Disease-causing microorganisms.

pedigree analysis: A diagram that shows the occurrence and appearance or phenotypes of a particular characteristic from one generation to the next.

period: The name given to the rows on the periodic table. The period number tells you how many 'electron shells' an atom has.

periodic table: A table displaying all the chemical elements, arranged in order of their atomic number.

peripheral nervous system (PNS): This consists of all the nerves not found in the CNS (brain and spinal cord).

perpendicular: At right angles to.

pH scale: Scale showing how strongly acidic or alkaline a solution is. Acids have a pH lower than 7; neutral solutions have a pH of 7; alkaline solutions have a pH above 7.

phenotype: This is the physical appearance of an offspring.

phloem: Transport tissue that carries dissolved food, mainly sugar, around a plant.

photosynthesis: Process by which plants make food (glucose) using carbon dioxide, water and light energy.

potential energy: Stored energy.

power: The energy transferred or transformed per second.

product: A substance formed after a chemical reaction has taken place.

proton: A subatomic particle with a positive charge, found in the nucleus of an atom.

Punnett square: A genetic diagram showing the possible offspring from a genetic cross.

R

radiation: Energy emitted from an object.

radioactive tracer: A radioactive isotope that is used to diagnose medical conditions. It is carried around the body in the bloodstream.

reactant: A substance you start with before a chemical reaction takes place.

receptors: Cells that detect changes in the environment.

recessive allele: The characteristic that these alleles code for will only show up in the offspring if both of the alleles inherited are recessive.

reflex action: Rapid, automatic response that occurs without thinking.

reflex arc: Neurone pathway from receptor to effector.

relative atomic mass: The mass of one atom of an element.

relay neurone: Neurone that links together a sensory neurone and a motor neurone.

renewable: An energy source that will never run out.

respiration: Process which releases energy from glucose in a living organism.

reversible reaction: A chemical reaction that can take place in both a forward and reverse direction.

ring main: A domestic wiring circuit.

root: Plant organ responsible for anchoring the plant into the ground and taking in water and nutrients.

S

salt: Metal compound made from an acid.

Sankey diagram: An energy transfer diagram.

sensory neurone: A neurone that carries impulses from a receptor to the CNS.

shiver: Rapid muscle contraction that generates heat (through respiration) to warm the body up.

specialised cell: Cells that are adapted to carry out a particular function.

speed of light: The speed at which all electromagnetic waves travel in a vacuum.

stem: Plant organ that supports the leaves and flowers.

stimulus: A change in the environment that is detected by receptors.

stomata: Openings in the leaves that allow gases to enter and leave the plant.

subatomic particle: Particles found within an atom – neutrons, protons and electrons.

sweat: A fluid consisting mainly of water that evaporates from the body to cool you down.

synapse: A gap between neurones, across which information has to be transmitted using chemicals.

T

target organ: Organ that a hormone causes its effect upon.

thermal: Alternative word for heat.

thermal imaging: A device that detects thermal energy and displays it as a visible image.

thymine: A DNA base that forms complementary bonds with adenine.

time period: Time taken to produce one wave, or for one wave to pass a fixed point.

tissue: A group of cells working together to perform a particular function.

toxins: Poisonous chemicals made by microorganisms.

transpiration: When water evaporates from plant cells into the air spaces in leaves. The water then diffuses out of the leaf through the stomata.

transpiration stream: The constant movement of water from the roots to the leaves through the xylem of a plant.

transverse: A type of wave, where the vibrations are perpendicular to the direction of wave motion.

U

ultrasound: Sound waves above the range of human hearing – above 20 kHz.

unit (of electricity): Equivalent to 1 kWh – the energy transferred when a 1 kW device is used for 1 hour.

universal indicator: A mixture of indicators that produces a number of colour changes depending on the pH of a solution.

useful energy: Energy transferred by a device, which is the intended output.

V

vacuole: Component of a plant cell that contains cell sap.

vacuum: A region containing no particles.

vasoconstriction: This is when blood vessels supplying capillaries in the skin narrow, reducing blood flow through the capillaries, reducing heat loss.

vasodilation: This is when blood vessels supplying capillaries in the skin widen, increasing blood flow through the capillaries, increasing heat loss.

visible spectrum: The frequencies of the electromagnetic spectrum that can be detected by the human eye.

voluntary response: This is when you make a conscious decision to do something.

W

wasted energy: Energy transferred by a device that is an unplanned output.

wavelength: The distance from one peak of a wave to the adjacent one.

word equation: Description of the reactants and products in a chemical reaction.

work done: Energy transferred or transformed.

X

xylem: Plant transport tissue that carries water around the plant.

Index

A

acid 58, 59, 61–7
    reacting with carbonates 63
    reacting with metals 62
adenine 10
alkali 58–9, 61, 65, 66, 67
allele 11–19
    dominant allele 12–15, 19
    recessive allele 12–15, 18, 19
amplitude 92, 93
animal cells 2–3, 4
answer questions, how to 109
antacid 58, 67
antibodies 2
atom 57, 68, 70, 112
    electron shells 48
    isotopes 46–7
    periodic table 50, 54–5
    structure 38–43
    word equation 71
atomic nucleus 39–40
    see also nucleus (atom)
atomic number 41–3, 45–9, 52, 112
atomic symbols 40

B

balanced equation 57
base 58, 59, 61, 67
battery 88
biofuel 84
blood cells 2
blood glucose concentration 32–3
body temperature 34

C

carbon dioxide, testing for 64
carbon neutral 84
carbonate 57, 63–4, 66, 68
carriers 14–15, 16, 18–19
cell membrane 3, 4, 5
cell wall 4, 5
cells 4
    adaptation 2–3
    components 4–5
    function 2–3
    structure 2–3
central nervous system (CNS) 2, 25–6
chemical bonds 55, 74, 75
chemical energy 74, 86, 88
chemical equation 57, 61–2
chemical formula 40, 54, 68
chemical symbol 49, 52, 54, 57
chloroplast 4, 5, 7
chromosome 11

clones 10
compound 54, 55–8, 63
    naming 56
conduction 76, 77
conductor 38, 77
convection current 75, 77
cystic fibrosis, pedigree analysis 15
cytoplasm 3, 4, 5
cytosine 10

D

dense 64, 77, 101
dissipate 79
DNA 10–11, 20
dominant allele 12–15, 19

E

effectors 2, 26–9
efficiency 83, 87, 113
egg cell 3
elastic potential energy 75
electrical energy, formulae 113
electricity cost 82
electricity, domestic 82
electromagnetic spectrum 96–7, 99,
    100–4, 106
electron shells 39, 48–50
electronic configuration 48–50
electrons 112
    atomic structure 39–40, 42–3
    electron shells 48–50
    isotopes 46
element 38, 40–3, 45–50, 54–5
endocrine system 31–4
energy forms 72–3
energy source 75, 84, 86, 87
energy store 73, 74–5, 84–8
energy transfers 76–7, 79–82
    conservation of energy 79
    electricity cost 82
    power 81
    radiation 76, 77, 92
    Sankey diagram 80
engulf 2

F

flammable 64, 66
fluid 77
fluorescent 101
formulae
    electrical energy 113
    scientific units 112
fossil fuels 72, 86, 87, 88

frequency 101–3, 112, 113
    electromagnetic spectrum 96–7, 99,
      106
    waves 92–3, 94–5, 96–7, 99, 106
fuel cell 74, 88

G

gamma camera 102
gamma rays 96, 97, 102, 104
gene 11, 12, 15, 17, 20
gene mutation 20, 104
genetic diagram 12–13, 16, 23
genetically inherited disorder 15, 18–19
genetics 112
genotype 16–17, 19
    pedigree analysis 17
geothermal energy 85
glands 24, 26, 27, 31, 34
glucagon 32–3
glycogen 32–3
gravitational potential energy 74, 79
group, periodic table 45, 50
guanine 10
guard cell 3

H

haemoglobin 2
hazard symbol 66
heterozygous 11, 14, 15, 16, 19
homeostasis 24, 31, 34
homozygous 11, 14, 15, 16, 19
hormones 6, 24, 27, 31–3
    vs. nerves 32
hydroelectric power 85
hydrogen, testing for 64

I

indicator 59, 61, 65
indigestion 67
infrared 76–7, 92, 96–7, 100, 103
insulator 27, 77
insulin 32–3
inversely proportional 95, 97
involuntary response 26, 28
irradiation 102
isotopes 46–7, 112

J

joule 79, 81, 112

K

kilowatt-hour 82
kinetic energy 72–4, 77, 79, 84–6, 90

L

law of conservation of energy 79, 80
leaf 3, 7, 8
liming 67
litmus paper 65
longitudinal 92, 93
luminous 72

M

mass number 42–3, 46–7, 52, 112
mesophyll 7
metal 38, 56, 58, 61–4, 77, 99
    reacting with acids 62
microwaves 99, 103
mitochondria 3, 4, 5
mixture 55
molecule 10, 40, 47, 54–5, 57, 68
monohybrid inheritance 12–13
motor neurone 2, 25–9
mutate 104
mutation 20, 104

N

National Grid 76
nerves 24–5, 27, 31, 32
    see also motor neurone; relay
        neurone; sensory neurone
    vs. hormones 32
nervous system 25–9
    central nervous system (CNS) 2,
        25–6
    peripheral nervous system (PNS)
        25
neurones see motor neurone; nerves;
    relay neurone; sensory neurone
neutral 42–3, 59, 61, 65
neutralisation 61, 63, 67
neutron 40, 42–3, 46, 112
newton 79
non-metal 38, 56
non-renewable 86, 87
nuclear decay 75
nuclear fission 73, 75, 87
nucleus (atom) 39–42, 46, 48, 73
nucleus (cell) 4, 5, 10, 11, 12

O

optical fibre 100
organ 6, 7
organ system 6
organism 6, 11, 20
oscillate 92, 93
oscillations 92–4, 96
oxidation 88

P

pathogens 2

pedigree analysis 14–15, 23
    cystic fibrosis 15
    genotype 17
    phenotype 17
period, periodic table 45, 50
periodic table 38, 40–1, 43, 47–50, 52,
    54
peripheral nervous system (PNS) 25
perpendicular 92, 93
pH scale 59, 65
phenotype 16–17, 19
    pedigree analysis 17
phloem 3, 7
photosynthesis 3, 4, 5, 7, 8
plant cells 3, 5
plant organs 7
polydactyly 19
potential energy 72–5, 79, 90
power 82, 84–7, 88, 113
    energy transfers 81
probability 18–19, 112
product, chemical reaction 56–8
proton 40–3, 46, 48–9, 112
Punnett square 12–13, 16, 23

R

radiation 96, 97, 100–4, 107
    energy transfers 76, 77, 92
    heat loss 34
    mutation 20
radio waves 96-7, 99
radioactive tracer 102
reactant, chemical reaction 56, 57,
    62–3
reagent 68
receptors 2, 26–9, 34
recessive allele 12–15, 18, 19
red blood cell 2
reflex action 28–9
reflex arc 29
relative atomic mass 42, 112
    isotopes 46–7
relay neurone 29
renewable energy sources 84–5, 90
respiration 4, 32
reversible reaction 88
revise, how to 108
ring main 76
root 3, 7, 8
root hair cell 3

S

salt 54, 58, 61, 62–3
Sankey diagram, energy transfers 80
science skills 110–11
scientific units, formulae 112
sensory neurone 2, 25–9
shiver 34
sickle-cell anaemia 18–19
solar energy 84

specialised cell 2, 6, 100
speed of light 93, 96
sperm cell 3
stem 7
stimulus 26–9
stomata 3, 8
subatomic particle 39–40, 42–3
sweat 34
synapse 26–7, 29

T

target organ 24, 31
thermal energy 72–4, 76–7, 79–80,
    83–7, 100
thermal imaging 72, 100
thymine 10
tidal power 85
time period 94–5, 113
tissue 6
    plant 7
toxins 2, 6
transpiration 8
transpiration stream 8
transverse 92, 93

U

ultrasound 73
ultraviolet (UV) radiation 101, 104
unit (of electricity) 82
universal indicator 61, 65
useful energy 79, 83, 113

V

vacuole 3, 4, 5
vacuum 93, 96
vasoconstriction 34
vasodilation 34
visible light 100
visible spectrum 97, 106
voluntary response 26

W

wasted energy 79, 80, 83, 90
wave power 85
wavelength 92–7, 99, 100–1, 106, 112,
    113
waves
    calculations 94–5, 113
    characteristics 92–3
    frequency 92–3, 94–5, 96–7, 99, 106
white blood cell 2
wind energy 84
word equation 56, 57, 61–3, 71
work done 76

X

X-rays 101, 104
xylem 3, 7, 8